WHAT IS CHRISTIANITY?

A concise, comprehensive,
non-denominational, and understandable
course of Bible study

by EDWIN ROELS

Forward by

Henry Reyenga

What is Christianity? Copyright © 2021 by Christian Leaders Publishing
Published by Christian Leaders Publishing
Spring Lake, Michigan

ISBN-13: 9798585928802

DEDICATION:

This book is dedicated to Mr. Ed VanDrunen, a long-time dear friend and ministry partner of Dr. Edwin Roels. Together these two men had the vision to seek first the Kingdom of God and collaborated to bring the Gospel to people all around the world.

Christian Leaders Ministries received permission to publish the works of Dr. Edwin Roels.

Contents

Forward

A Two by Two Ministry Adventure

After this, the Lord appointed seventy-two others and sent them two by two ahead of him to every town and place where he was about to go. He told them, "The harvest is plentiful, but the workers are few. Ask the Lord of the harvest, therefore, to send out workers into his harvest field." <u>Luke 10:1-2</u>

Toward the close of the 20th century, God sent out two Eds. Ed Roels and Ed VanDrunen often served as a team to raise up more Christian leaders. Together, they ministered in places throughout Africa and Asia (such as Myanmar and India), as well as Russia and Ukraine.

Dr. Ed Roels was a pastor called into full-time ministry. He also served as a professor, chaplain to servicemen in Korea, president of Reformed Bible College (now called Kuyper College) and in global ministry training as African Director of the World Home Bible League.

Mr. Ed VanDrunen was a farmer and businessman who served as an elder in his local church. While actively working with the farming operations of VanDrunen Farms, he was also active in his community and local Christian schools and served on numerous ministry boards (including Christian Leaders).

The two Eds met at their church in Illinois where Dr. Roels was the pastor and Mr. VanDrunen was one of the elders. Pastor Roels had the ability to explain complicated biblical subjects simply and with clarity.

It was not long after their meeting that the two men began ministering beyond their church in South Holland, Illinois. This pastor/farmer ministry team was sent out as "workers into his harvest field."

Spreading Christianity in India and Beyond

On one of their ministry travels, they met with a pastor in India named Mano Daniel. Pastor Daniel ran a ministry that raised up volunteer, part-time, and full-time Christian leaders and ministers.

As their teaching and mentoring mission concluded on that visit, Pastor Daniel requested that Dr. Roels write a clear and concise study on the Christian faith in English. He would then translate the material into Tamil and Hindi. In response to this request and supported by his ministry friend, Dr. Roels accepted this challenge and worked towards the writing and production of a four part Christian Basics series.

The completed Bible study books include:

The Path to Eternal Life

Talking to God

Walking with God

By Grace Alone

Various global ministries began using these books, which were eventually also translated into Tamil, Hindi, Chinese, Spanish, Ukrainian, Russian and French languages.

The *What is Christianity?* book is a result of these efforts and is a summary of *The Path to Eternal Life* book from the Christian Basics series.

Spreading Christian Training at the Christian Leaders Institute

Ed Van Drunen introduced the material to the Christian Leaders Institute shortly after it was founded in 2006. Van Drunen served as a founding board member. Christian Leaders Institute was set up to offer free, generosity supported ministry training for new Christians and volunteer, part-time, or full-time ministers.

How can this Christianity study help you grow or influence others?

New Christians: If you are a new or recent convert to Christianity, this study will give you the foundational knowledge of Christianity to better understand the Bible and grow in your faith.

Christian Parents: This clear and concise understanding of Christianity will help you lead and disciple your children in the faith.

Ministry Leaders: If you are serving as a ministry leader in a local church or your community, this study will give you confidence that you know the essential teachings of Christianity.

Ordained Leaders: If you are serving as an ordained leader such as a deacon or elder, this study will help you serve your local church as you grow in your leadership competency.

Ordained Ministers: If you are a licensed or ordained minister or pastor, this study will be an excellent tool for sharing Christianity or discipling others.

Mission Inspiration

These two Eds have inspired countless thousands of Christians by going two by two. Our prayer for you as you consider doing this study is to pair up with someone. Maybe do this study with your spouse or a friend. Maybe start a Bible study. You will never know where the Lord will take you as you hear his call! Remember, "The harvest is plentiful, but the workers are few. Ask the Lord of the harvest, therefore, to send out workers into his harvest field."

Do you desire a formal study that will deepen your knowledge of Christianity?

Christian Leaders Institute offers free online ministry training courses. This Bible study is the textbook for the "THE 101 - Christian Basics: Introduction to Christian Doctrine" course. Visit www.christianleadersinstitute.org.

Introduction

For millions of people life on this earth is very difficult. Day after day they face sickness and sadness, poverty and hunger, disappointment and frustration, dishonesty and injustice. Even the rich and the powerful have to deal with at least some of these things. No one is totally beyond the reach of failures and frustrations, floods and storms, disease and death. Everyone dies eventually, whether rich or poor, young or old, wise or foolish leaving everything behind.

All this leads many people to wonder: Is this really all there is to life? Will things always be this way? Is there no hope for the future? Must we all just struggle to make our way through this broken world and then someday leave this world to plunge into an unknown future?

By studying this course you will discover that there *is* meaning to this present life and there *is* a sure hope for the future. This course will not deceive you into believing that you can live on this earth without any trials or frustrations or disappointments. But it will teach you how you can begin to enjoy a joyful and meaningful life already now and how you can enjoy an eternal life of love and joy and peace when your earthly life is over.

If this is something you would like to know more about, we encourage you to faithfully read and study each Lesson in this course.

In this Introduction to the course, you will find a brief overview of the main teachings of the entire course. Each of these teachings will be explained at greater length in the lessons that follow. By getting an overview of the entire course from the very beginning, you will be able to understand more clearly how each teaching fits as a part of the whole picture. It's like seeing the picture of a completed puzzle before you try to put each of the pieces together.

Overview: The Basic Teachings of Each Lesson

Lesson One: The Bible

Though people honor and worship many different gods or idols, there is only one true God in this world. We learn about this God in various ways. God has made himself known to us through his marvelous creation, through the voice of conscience within us, and through his mighty works throughout history.

However, we can learn much more about God through *the written Word* which he gave us. This written Word not only teaches us many things about God, but it also teaches us how to live our lives in a way that most pleases him. God's written Word is known to us as *The Bible*.

Lesson Two: God

The Bible teaches us many things about God. Though we cannot perfectly understand everything God teaches us in the Bible, we can learn everything we need to know in order for us to love him, serve him and trust him. The God of the Bible is a God of love, holiness, justice, compassion, and mercy. He has neither beginning nor end. He knows everything about everyone and can do anything that he chooses to do. He is not a physical being like we are but is a perfect, invisible Spirit who is present everywhere.

Lesson Three: Origins

In the beginning of time, God created the earth and the rest of the world out of nothing. After he had created all the plants and animals, he created human beings to rule over the earth, to take care of it, and to enjoy it. The earth was initially a beautiful place, free from all forms of evil, sin, and destruction. After a while, however, the people that God created chose to disobey him and tried to become equal with him. Because of their sin and disobedience, God punished them as he said he would.

5

After the first people sinned, they lost the unbroken joy and fellowship they had with God in the beginning. Instead of enjoying peace and harmony, they experienced suffering, sickness, trouble, sorrow, and death. In addition, the entire creation began to experience ruin and decay.

However, God did not leave people without hope. He promised that someday he would send a Savior into the world. This Savior would pay the penalty for man's sin and would pave the way for the creation of a beautiful new world in which everyone who trusted in the promised Savior would enjoy eternal peace and love and joy.

Lesson Four: Jesus Christ

Though God revealed many things about himself in the Bible, he revealed himself to us most fully by sending his only Son into the world. This Son is the Savior whom God promised to send to the earth after people fell into sin. Though the Son was fully God like his Father, he came to earth in the form of a human being and was born to a young Jewish virgin named Mary.

When he was born, he was given the name *Jesus* which means *Savior* or *God Saves*. Jesus is also called *Christ*, which means *the anointed one*, since he was anointed by God the Holy Spirit. As the God-Man, Jesus was the only person who ever lived a perfect life. However, in spite of his perfect and sinless life, Jesus was hated by many of his countrymen and was eventually crucified outside the city of Jerusalem.

But three days later he rose again from the dead! For forty days he visited with his followers and then returned again to Heaven from where he now rules over the entire world.

Lesson Five: Salvation

After reading the wonderful story of Jesus, it may still not be clear to you just what Jesus accomplished while he was here on earth. Jesus is called the Savior, but the world still seems to be lost.

6

Suffering and sorrow abound, and people continue to die as they always have. Even the natural world around us suffers from ruin and decay. In some ways life seems to be getting worse rather than better. So what does it mean that Jesus saves?

In this lesson we learn how Jesus paid the penalty for the sins of all who put their trust in him as their Savior. God graciously forgives their sins and gives them the gift of eternal life. When believers die physically (as all people do), their spirits are taken immediately into the presence of Jesus in heaven while their bodies await a future resurrection.

Lesson Six: The Holy Spirit

While Jesus was still on earth, he promised his followers that he would send the Holy Spirit of God to them when he returned to heaven. Up to that point Jesus' followers (called disciples) knew very little about the Holy Spirit. So Jesus explained to them who the Holy Spirit is, how the Spirit would come to them, and how he would empower them to live as Jesus had taught them.

The Holy Spirit would also serve as their counselor and guide, bringing to their minds everything Jesus had taught them while he was on earth. And through the Holy Spirit in their hearts, believers would be able to produce spiritual fruit that would glorify God the Father.

Lesson Seven: Christian Living

Some people are eager to receive the salvation Jesus gives, but have many questions about what it means to live as a Christian. They seem to think that Christian living is primarily a matter of dos and don'ts and are afraid that Christianity will take all the fun out of their lives. But that is definitely not true.

Christians certainly should stay away from everything that displeases or dishonors God, but the basic rule of Christian living is that we love God above everything else and that we love others as ourselves. We may often fail to live and love as God wants us to, but through the work of the Holy Spirit in our hearts we will increasingly do the will of God and find joy in doing so.

Lesson Eight: Prayer

One of the greatest privileges believers have as they seek to live a Christian life is prayer. Prayer is simply communicating with God through our thoughts and words. When we pray sincerely, we are speaking directly and personally with our Father in heaven who always hears us. We do not have to use special words or formulas or a special tone of voice, but simply and sincerely bring our deepest feelings and desires directly to God. Through prayer we express our needs, confess our sins, bring our thanks, and enjoy fellowship with the one who created us and saved us and loves us.

Lesson Nine: Marriage and Family

Christian faith affects every area of our lives and every choice we make. Of special importance is marriage and family life where our joys can be the greatest but where tensions and frustrations can be the strongest. The Bible therefore teaches us many things about the proper relationship between husbands and wives and between parents and their children.

Lesson Ten: Suffering and Persecution

Christians who live on this earth are not yet free from trials, problems, failures, sickness, disappointments, or even from sin. In addition, Christians often suffer persecution or opposition because of their faith. But God is faithful to all his promises and will forgive those who sincerely repent of their sins and seek to live a life that is pleasing to him. God has also promised that he will never leave or forsake those who love him and put their trust in him. So, even in the midst of their failures and trials, Christians continue to love and serve and trust their Savior and look forward to the time when they will live forever with him in glory.

Lesson Eleven: The Future

When believers die, their spirits immediately go to be with Jesus Christ in heaven, where they await the time when Jesus will return to earth and raise up the bodies of all those who have died. God will create a new world in which believers will live forever in glory, joy and praise. It is impossible for us now to fully understand how wonderful and beautiful it will be to spend eternity with our Lord and with other believers from all over the world. However, we know that it will be even more glorious than anything we can even imagine. We shall give thanks and praise to God for ever and ever and enjoy a life that is perfect in every way.

Lesson One: The Bible

Introduction

Most people in the world believe there is a Higher Power of some kind who is far greater than any person on earth. People have different ideas, however, as to who or what this Higher Power is. Some people do not believe in a personal God at all. Others believe that there are hundreds or even millions of gods. The Bible, however, teaches that there is only one true God and that He alone is worthy of our worship and our praise.

But you may ask, "Why should I trust what the Bible says?" That's a fair question! It may not be possible to prove to you that the Bible is truly the Word of God, but there are some very good reasons why millions of people do believe that it is. Among those reasons are the following.

Reasons to Believe that the Bible is the Word of God

1. No other book in the entire world is as old, as trustworthy and as comprehensive as the Bible is in teaching us about God, ourselves, and the future. The Bible begins with the story of the creation of the world and ends with the promise of a new world where there will be no sin, no sickness, no suffering and no death. And in between the accounts of the world's wonderful beginning and its glorious future, the Bible gives us the history of man's life on earth, including his fall into sin and his salvation from sin. It also tells us many of the marvelous works of God through the course of human history.
2. The writers of the Bible taught and believed that their writings were inspired by God. Jesus Christ, who is honored and trusted by more people than anyone who has ever lived on this earth, also believed and taught that the Bible is truly the Word of God.
3. The Bible provides answers to many of our sincere questions about God, our world and ourselves which we cannot find anywhere else. Neither nature nor history nor philosophy nor any other book provides the answers which our minds and hearts are

looking for.

4. The Bible not only teaches us what is right and what is wrong in the sight of God, it also teaches us how we can gain the power to do what is right and overcome what is wrong.

5. The Bible has many prophecies concerning individuals, nations, and specific events. Many of these prophecies have already been fulfilled exactly as they were foretold. Since many of the Bible's prophecies have already been fulfilled in the past, we can also trust what it teaches about the future.

6. The Bible contains sixty-six different books or documents which were written over a period of 1500 years by forty different men who lived on three different continents. However, each part of the Bible, when properly understood, agrees with all the other parts.

7. Scholars have carefully studied archeological findings and other historical materials which confirm the accuracy of the Bible's teachings about geography and history. Though the Bible is very old, it is clearly a very trustworthy book in everything it records.

8. We have more ancient copies of the Bible (or parts of the Bible) than any other book that has ever been written. We can have complete confidence that the Bible we have today is essentially unchanged from the time it was first written. There is no other ancient book like it.

9. The Bible has been the most influential book in the history of the world. It was the first book ever printed. It has been translated into more languages than any other book. It has been distributed more widely than any other book. And God has preserved it from every attempt of people to destroy it.

10. Millions of people have been dramatically changed for good through reading, studying, and believing what the Bible teaches. The Bible does not simply give us information about things that happened in the past. It gives us guidelines for living in the present and provides us with encouragement and hope regarding the future. It teaches us how we can find forgiveness, happiness and peace in our present life and shows us the way to an eternal life of glory, delight and joy in the presence of the one true God who created us and loves us.

QUESTIONS ABOUT THE BIBLE

1. Where did the Bible come from?

Every book of the Bible has a human author, but God himself was the ultimate author. According to 2 Timothy 3:16, the Bible is "God-breathed." This means that God supernaturally "breathed out" his message through the human writers in such a way that the words they wrote were truly the words of God himself. Sometimes God spoke to the writers directly. Sometimes he dictated things to them. At other times he helped them to search out the truth so that they could share it with others. At all times he guided them in such a way that they wrote down in their own personal styles the things he wanted them to write. He also kept them from making errors in all that they wrote.

Scripture References
All Scripture is breathed out by God and profitable for teaching, for reproof, for correction and for training in righteousness. (2 Timothy 3:16)
For no prophecy was ever produced by the will of man, but men spoke from God as they were carried along by the Holy Spirit. (2 Peter 1:21)

2. What can we gain by studying the Bible?

a. The Bible teaches us many important truths that we cannot learn anywhere else.
b. The Bible introduces us to the real, living God.
c. The Bible teaches us how to live in a way that honors and pleases God.
d. The Bible promises us many wonderful blessings if we follow its teachings.
e. The Bible shows us how we may have an everlasting life full of joy and peace.

Scripture References

Man shall not live by bread alone, but by every word that comes from the mouth of God. (Matthew 4:4)
I have stored up your word in my heart that I might not sin against you. (Psalm 119:11)
The rules of the LORD are true . . . In keeping them there is great reward. (Psalm 19:9-11)
Blessed is the man . . . whose delight is in the law of the LORD . . . He is like a tree planted by streams of water that yields its fruit in its season, and its leaf does not wither. In all that he does, he prospers. (Psalm 1:1-3)

3. Can we trust what the Bible says?

Yes! God's Word is true in every way and all its promises will be fulfilled. We should recognize, however, that some parts of the Bible were written in a poetic style or with figures of speech that should not be interpreted literally.

Scripture References
For the word of the LORD is upright. (Psalm 33:4)
All his precepts are trustworthy. (Psalm 111:7)
The sum of your word is truth; and every one of your righteous rules endures forever. (Psalm 119:160)

4. What did Jesus teach about the Bible?

When Jesus lived on earth, the New Testament had not yet been written. However, he quoted from the Old Testament, recognized it as the true Word of God, taught that it was completely trustworthy, said that all its prophecies would surely be fulfilled, and declared that the Scriptures were pointing to himself.

Scripture References
Jesus said: *"Your Word is truth." (John 17:17)*
Jesus said: *"Until heaven and earth pass away, not an iota, not a dot, will pass from the Law until all is accomplished." (Matthew 5:18)*

Jesus said, *"Scripture cannot be broken." (John 10:35)*
Jesus said, *"You diligently study the Scriptures because you think that by them you possess eternal life. These are the Scriptures that testify about me." (John 5:39)*
Beginning with Moses and all the Prophets, he [Jesus] explained to them in all the Scriptures the things concerning himself. (Luke 24:27)

5. Since the Bible was written many years ago, can it still be of help to us today?

Absolutely! The Bible is a living book which speaks to the hearts of people in every age, in every place and in every situation. Its truths continue to be a guide, an inspiration, a comfort, and a challenge to people around the world.

Scripture References
For the word of God is living and active, sharper than any two-edged sword, piercing to the division of soul and of spirit, of joints and of marrow, and discerning the thoughts and intentions of the heart. (Hebrews 4:12)
All Scripture is breathed out by God and profitable for teaching, for reproof, for correction, and for training in righteousness, that the man of God may be complete, equipped for every good work. (2 Timothy 3:16-17)

6. How can the Bible be a guide for us?

The Bible teaches us what is right and what is wrong in the sight of God. It also gives us important moral guidelines for every area of life—marriage, family, work, education, recreation, leisure, business, politics, and personal relationships. Though the Bible does not deal with every possible situation that may arise, it does give us general principles which can be helpful throughout our entire lives no matter where we live or what we are doing.

Scripture References
How can a young man keep his way pure? By guarding it according to your word. (Psalm 119:9)

14

Your word is a lamp to my feet and a light to my path. (Psalm 119:105)
When I think on my ways, I turn my feet to your testimonies. (Psalm 119:59)
For the commandment is a lamp and the teaching a light, and the reproofs of discipline are the way of life. (Proverbs 6:23)

7. What are some of the other ways the Bible can help us in our everyday life?

The Bible provides us with comfort in times of sorrow, encouragement in times of special need, hope in times of distress, inspiration in times of personal challenge, peace in times of turmoil, and assurance of God's loving presence at all times.

Scripture References
The law of the Lord is perfect, reviving the soul. (Psalm 19:7)
The precepts of the LORD are right, rejoicing the heart. (Psalm 19:8)
Great peace have those who love your law; nothing can make them stumble. (Psalm 119:165)
I will never forget your precepts, for by them you have given me life. (Psalm 119:93)
This is my comfort in my affliction, that your promise gives me life. (Psalm 119:50)
Whatever was written in former days was written for our instruction, that through endurance and through the encouragement of the Scriptures we might have hope. (Romans 15:4)

8. What is the greatest benefit we can receive from reading and studying the Bible?

The greatest benefit we can receive through reading, studying and believing the Bible is knowing God and finding the way to eternal life through faith in Jesus. All other blessings we receive in this life may be temporary, but the life we receive through faith in Jesus is eternal and glorious.

Scripture References

From childhood you have been acquainted with the sacred writings, which are able to make you wise for salvation through faith in Christ Jesus. (2 Timothy 3:15)

These are written so that you may believe that Jesus is the Christ, the Son of God, and that by believing you may have life in his name. (John 20:31)

Exploring Further

1. What difference would it make in your life if you did not have a Bible or know what the Bible teaches?

For most of us, life would be very different. We would not know where we came from, where we are going, or how we should be living in order to honor and please God. We would not have the peace and joy that come from knowing Jesus. We would not have the comfort of knowing that God loves us, cares for us, forgives us, understands our weaknesses, and is preparing an eternal home for us in glory. We would not have the blessing of knowing how God wants us to live or what he wants us to do. We would basically be wandering in a broken world with few trustworthy guidelines for the present and very little hope for the future.

2. Why is it important that we can trust what the Bible says?

If we cannot trust what the Bible says, we will continue to live in confusion and uncertainty. There would be no authoritative answer for any of our questions. We would always wonder whether our own thoughts and ideas are right or wrong. And we would have no sure way to judge or evaluate the thoughts and ideas of others. We would continue to live day after day wondering whether our thoughts and ideas were really true or simply the product of our own desires and imagination.

3. In what ways does the Old Testament help us understand the New Testament?

The Old Testament gives us the story of creation, the story of man's fall into sin, God's first promises of redemption, and the history of God's people during the centuries before the coming of Jesus. The Old Testament gives us a clear picture of humanity's sinful nature and inability to earn or merit salvation and forgiveness by keeping the laws God gave to his people. It gives us a very clear presentation of human weakness and God's greatness, man's unfaithfulness and God's faithfulness.

Without the Old Testament, we could not fully understand our sinfulness and our inability to obtain salvation on our own, nor could we as fully understand the majesty, power, mercy, and grace of God. Jesus was born into the family line of the Old Testament figures such as Abraham, Isaac, Jacob (Israel), Judah and David. Jesus fulfilled the wonderful promises God made to Adam at the dawn of human history, and he also met all the demands and requirements God presented in the Old Testament hundreds of years before. It is impossible to fully understand who Jesus was, why he came, and what he did unless we also know at least some of the teachings of the Old Testament.

4. Are the words of Jesus recorded in the Bible more trustworthy or more important than other parts of the Bible?

No. In some Bibles the words of Jesus are printed in red letters to set these words apart from others. And in some ways that may be helpful. To know what Jesus said and taught can be very helpful. However, it's important to remember that EVERY word in the Bible has been inspired by the Holy Spirit and is therefore trustworthy. At the same time, it's also important to recognize that some passages in the Bible are more significant than others in helping us learn the way of salvation and helping us learn how God wants us to live. For example, Jesus' Sermon on the Mount in Matthew 5-7 and Paul's teachings in Romans 12 are much more helpful for teaching us God's will for our lives than some other passages are.

5. What is meant by "progressive revelation"?

"Progressive revelation" is the term used to describe the fact that God gradually gave people new information concerning himself and his laws and his plan of salvation. The information which he gave at every point was true and trustworthy, but later on he often gave additional information about himself, his will, his plans, and his purposes.

So, for example, people in Old Testament times did not know that the God they served was a Trinity of Father, Son, and Spirit. Neither did they know that God would someday come to this earth in the form of a man (Jesus) who would die on the cross for the sins of the world. And they did not understand that someday both Jews and non-Jews would have an equal status before God as they were joined together in Jesus Christ. Because the Bible contains progressive revelation on many subjects, we should be very careful not to read an early passage in the Bible as God's final and complete revelation on a subject.

6. Since the Bible is a very old book, shouldn't we look to newer books for better and more accurate information about God and the world?

The fact that the Bible is very old is actually something positive and not negative. In spite of the fact that the Bible has existed for so many years, it continues to be printed and translated and sold around the world in very large numbers. This by itself is an indication that the Bible is a most unusual book and worthy of careful study. Though there are some people who may reject it, the Bible still is the most influential book in the world. It continues to be a source of comfort, challenge, inspiration, information and life-changing power. It does not claim to be a textbook on science or mathematics or other subjects of that kind, but it does teach eternal truths about God, salvation, and the way to eternal life.

We should be careful not to use the Bible as a textbook on subjects (such as science) which we can explore ourselves, but we should recognize that the Bible goes beyond science to reveal that God is the creator and sustainer of our incredible world filled with all its marvels and mysteries.

7. What is the strongest reason for believing what the Bible says?

There are many strong reasons, but the most important reason is that the Holy Spirit impresses on your mind and heart that the Bible is truly the Word of God.

8. Is it confusing or is it helpful to have more than one translation of the Bible in your language?

Since no single translation is absolutely perfect, there are advantages in reading the Bible in different versions. Some early versions were not done especially well, so these older versions can be corrected by new and more accurate versions. Further, language changes somewhat over the years, so an older version may contain language which is no longer used among the common people and will not be easily understood.

In addition, by reading a different version, students may be led to look at a passage in a new way which they had not thought of before. They may also find that a strictly literal translation does not always helpfully represent the original text. For example, because each language has figures of speech of one kind or another, a strictly literal translation could be misleading. On the other hand, by having only one version of the Bible in a given language, everyone has the advantage of learning and memorizing and quoting exactly the same words. And that can be a very significant benefit!

9. What is the best way to respond to people who believe and teach the Bible has been changed and corrupted over the years?

Perhaps the best way to respond is to begin by asking them some questions. For example: (1) Why do you believe that the Bible has been changed or corrupted? (2) Who do you think made the changes? (3) Why did these people decide to make these changes? (4) When were the alleged changes made? (5) What happened to the original manuscripts of the Bible? (6) What proof do you have that the alleged changes were made? (If the originals no longer exist, how do we know that the Bible has been changed or corrupted?)

There are differences in some of the thousands of Bible manuscripts in existence. Most of these, however, are very minor and of little significance. Besides, most scholars who have made it their primary work to study the ancient Bible manuscripts agree that we can be very confident that there is nothing in the original Bible manuscripts that has been lost—even though we no longer have the originals themselves. Without any legitimate doubt, the Bible is extremely accurate and completely trustworthy.

10. What are some of the most fruitful ways to study the Bible and learn what it teaches?

We should read a portion of the Bible every day. We should try to find a time and a place to read the Bible where we will not be interrupted. We should ask the Holy Spirit (the author of the Bible) to help us understand what we read. We should, if possible, memorize at least something each time we read the Bible. We should immediately seek to put into practice the truths we have learned. We should seek to share what we have read or learned with someone else. We should read the Bible systematically and not simply jump from one part of the Bible to another. (For example, we might choose to read through an entire book of the Bible before going on to other parts of the Bible.) We should read something from both Old and New Testaments on a regular basis.

We should read from different parts of the Bible (such as Psalms, Proverbs, the Gospel accounts, the Epistles, etc.) on a regular basis rather than spending most of our Bible reading time in just one part of the Bible. We should seek to read with understanding rather than simply spending time reading the Bible without understanding it.

In this connection, we may wish to read a Bible commentary (if available) to help us understand what we are reading. Or, if we do not have access to a commentary, we might choose to ask someone else to help us understand what we have read. We should also make a definite effort to put into practice the truths we have read rather than simply reading them and then forgetting them. It can be helpful to write down in our own words some of the truths we have learned through our reading of the day.

Lesson Two: God

Introduction

For many people the word "God" does not mean very much. They do not know who God is or what he has done. They do not know whether there is only one God or many gods—or whether there is any God at all. They may have some general ideas about God and may even use his name in their ordinary conversation, but they definitely do not know him. And they aren't at all sure that it is even possible to know anything about him. They are not terrified by his awesome holiness, they are not afraid of his perfect justice, and they are not comforted by his gracious promises. They have no idea whether or not God knows any more about them than they know about him. And they have no idea how to find out. Whether God truly exists or not, he definitely does not have a significant place in their present life or in their plans for the future. In this Lesson you will learn some of the things the Bible teaches us about the one true God. Whether or not you believe what the Bible says, you will at least learn what the Bible teaches.

1. Who is God?

God is the Creator of the world and the source of all life.

Scripture References
The God who made the world and everything in it, being Lord of heaven and earth . . . gives to all mankind life and breath and everything. (Acts 17:24-25)
You are the LORD, you alone. You have made heaven, the heaven of heavens, with all their host, the earth and all that is on it, the seas and all that is in them; and you preserve all of them; and the host of heaven worships you. (Nehemiah 9:6)

2. How many true Gods are there?

There are millions of so-called "gods" in the world, but there

22

is only one true God who is worthy of our worship and praise.

Scripture References

I am the LORD, and there is no other; besides me there is no God. (Isaiah 45:5)
Thus says the LORD . . . the LORD of hosts: "I am the first and I am the last; besides me there is no god."(Isaiah 44:6)
Before me no god was formed, nor shall there be any after me. I, I am the LORD, and besides me there is no savior. (Isaiah 43:10-11)

3. How has God made himself known to us?

God has made himself known to people in many ways. One of the ways he has revealed himself to people around the world is through his work of creation.

Scripture References

The heavens declare the glory of God and the sky above proclaims his handiwork. Day to day pours out speech, and night to night reveals knowledge. There is no speech, nor are there words, whose voice is not heard. Their voice goes out through all the earth and their words to the end of the world. (Psalm 19:1-4)
His invisible attributes, namely, his eternal power and divine nature, have been clearly perceived, ever since the creation of the world, in the things that have been made. So they are without excuse. (Romans 1:20)

4. Is there any other way in which God has made himself known to us?

Yes. God frequently spoke to prophets and others so that they would know his will for their lives. He also provided them with comfort, encouragement, guidance, and other information that he wanted them to have. Those who received messages from God often wrote them down so that others could also benefit from them. Many of those written messages were collected together in The Holy Bible.

Scripture References

Long ago, at many times and in many ways, God spoke to our fathers by the prophets. (Hebrews 1:1)

Jesus said, "Everything written about me in the Law of Moses and the Prophets and the Psalms must be fulfilled." Then he opened their minds to understand the Scriptures. (Luke 24:44-45)

Jesus said, "The Helper, the Holy Spirit, whom the Father will send in my name, he will teach you all things and bring to your remembrance all that I have said to you." (John 14:26)

5. How has God revealed himself to us most clearly?

God has revealed himself most clearly and fully in his Son, Jesus Christ.

Scripture References

In these last days he [God] has spoken to us by his Son. (Hebrews 1:2)

No one has ever seen God; the only God, who is at the Father's side, he has made him known. (John 1:18)

[Jesus] is the image of the invisible God, the firstborn of all creation. (Colossians 1:15)

6. What does the Bible teach us about the holiness of God?

God himself is perfectly holy, free from imperfection or fault of any kind in his Person and in his dealings with others. Because of his own holiness, he also requires and demands that we also must be holy. Further, his holiness requires that all actions, thoughts, and words which are not holy must be punished in one way or another.

Scripture References

Holy, holy, holy is the LORD of hosts; the whole earth is full of his glory! (Isaiah 6:3)

Exalt the LORD . . . for the LORD our God is holy! (Psalm 99:9)

There is none holy like the LORD. (1 Samuel 2:2)

You who are of purer eyes than to see evil, and cannot look at wrong. (Habakkuk 1:13)

7. What does the Bible teach about the goodness and grace of God?

God gives us both material and spiritual blessings in abundance. All that we receive from him is given because of his kindness and grace and not because of anything we merit or deserve.

Scripture References
Bless the LORD, O my soul, and forget not all his benefits, who forgives all your iniquity, who heals all your diseases, who redeems your life from the pit, who crowns you with steadfast love and mercy, who satisfies you with good so that your youth is renewed like the eagle's. (Psalm 103:2-5)
The LORD is good to all, and his mercy is over all that he has made. (Psalm 145:9)
The LORD upholds all who are falling and raises up all who are bowed down. . . . He fulfills the desire of those who fear him; he also hears their cry and saves them. (Psalm 145:14, 19)
He did good by giving you rains from heaven and fruitful seasons, satisfying your hearts with food and gladness. (Acts14:17)

8. Does God forgive the sins of those who truly repent?

Yes. Though God himself is perfectly holy and wants us to live holy and obedient lives, he is also slow to anger, merciful, and forgiving. When we are genuinely sorry for our sins and ask him to forgive us, he graciously does so.

Scripture References
The LORD is merciful and gracious, slow to anger and abounding in steadfast love. He will not always chide, nor will he keep his anger forever. He does not deal with us according to our sins, nor repay us according to our iniquities. For as high as the heavens are above the earth, so great is his steadfast love toward

those who fear him; as far as the east is from the west, so far does he remove our transgressions from us. (Psalm 103:8-12)
You, O LORD, are a God merciful and gracious, slow to anger and abounding in steadfast love and faithfulness. (Psalm 86:15)
Who is a God like you, pardoning iniquity and passing over transgression? . . . He does not retain his anger forever, because he delights in steadfast love. (Micah 7:18)

9. Does God forgive those who do not love him or trust him or repent of their sins?

No. God is a God of mercy and love, but he is also a God of justice and holiness and will punish those who do not repent of their sins.

Scripture References
The LORD, the LORD, a God merciful and gracious, slow to anger and abounding in steadfast love and faithfulness, keeping steadfast love for thousands, forgiving iniquity and transgression and sin, but who will by no means clear the guilty. (Exodus 34:6-7)
Because of your hard and impenitent heart you are storing up wrath for yourself on the day of wrath when God's righteous judgment will be revealed. (Romans 2:5)
For you may be sure of this, that everyone who is sexually immoral or impure, or who is covetous (that is, an idolater), has no inheritance in the kingdom of Christ and God. Let no one deceive you with empty words, for because of these things the wrath of God comes upon the sons of disobedience. (Ephesians 5:5-6)

10. What does the Bible teach about the love of God?

Though God must punish the sins of those who do not truly repent, his love is far greater than we can measure or even imagine.

Scripture References
For as high as the heavens are above the earth, so great is his steadfast love for those who fear him. (Psalm 103:11)
For God so loved the world, that he gave his only Son, that whoever believes in him should not perish but have eternal life. (John 3:16)
For you, O LORD, are good and forgiving, abounding in steadfast love to all who call upon you. (Psalm 86:5)
God is love. (1 John 4:8)

11. Was there ever a time when God did not exist?

No. Though we cannot understand the eternity of God, the Bible clearly teaches that God did not have a beginning and he will never have an end. He is from everlasting to everlasting.

Scripture References
Before the mountains were brought forth, or ever you had formed the earth and the world, from everlasting to everlasting you are God. (Psalm 90:2)
The LORD is the everlasting God, the Creator of the ends of the earth. (Isaiah 40:28)
To the King of the ages, immortal, invisible, the only God, be honor and glory forever and ever. Amen. (1 Timothy 1:17)

12. Is it possible for us to see God?

No. At times God did assume a physical form which made him visible to people he was talking to, but he is an eternal spiritual being that cannot be seen by human eyes.

Scripture References
God is spirit, and those who worship him must worship in spirit and truth. (John 4:24)
No one has ever seen God. (1 John 4:12)
[God] dwells in unapproachable light, whom no one has ever seen or can see. (1 Timothy 6:16)

13. Is God's power limited in any way?

No. God is all powerful and is able to do whatever he chooses to do. This attribute of God is referred to as his "omnipotence."

Scripture References
Whatever the LORD pleases, he does, in heaven and on earth, in the seas and all deeps. (Psalm 135:6)
All things are possible with God. (Mark 10:27)
Our God is in the heavens; he does all that he pleases. (Psalm 115:3)
Ah, Lord GOD! It is you who have made the heavens and the earth by your great power and by your outstretched arm! Nothing is too hard for you. (Jeremiah 32:17)

14. Is God able to be in more than one place at the same time?

Yes. God is always present everywhere. This, too, is something we cannot fully comprehend, but the Bible makes it very clear that there is no place where we can hide from God or flee from God. This attribute of God is called his "omnipresence."

Scripture References
Where shall I go from your Spirit? Or where shall I flee from your presence? If I ascend to heaven, you are there! If I make my bed in Sheol, you are there! (Psalm 139:7-8)
The eyes of the LORD are in every place, keeping watch on the evil and the good. (Proverbs 15:3)
"Can a man hide himself in secret places so that I cannot see him?" declares the LORD. "Do I not fill heaven and earth?" (Jeremiah 23:24)

15. Is there anything that God does not know?

No. God knows everything about everyone everywhere. He not only knows what we say and do but he also knows our thoughts and desires. He knows the past as well as the future. There is absolutely nothing hidden from God. This attribute of God is called his "omniscience."

Scripture References

O LORD, you have searched me and known me. You know when I sit down and when I rise up; you discern my thoughts from afar. . . . You search out my path and my lying down and are acquainted with all my ways. Even before a word is on my tongue, behold, O LORD, you know it altogether. (Psalm 139:1-4)

I am God, and there is none like me. I make known the end from the beginning, from ancient times, what is still to come. (Isaiah 46:9-10)

God is greater than our heart, and he knows everything. (1 John 3:20)

No creature is hidden from his sight, but all are naked and exposed to the eyes of him to whom we must give account. (Hebrews 4:13)

16. Does God rule over the entire world or only part of it?

God is the sovereign Lord who rules over the entire world. Though there are many human rulers who exercise authority over parts of the world, God has ultimate authority over every person, every ruler, every kingdom and every nation. He has always been Lord over all and he always will be.

Scripture References

The LORD is God in heaven above and on the earth beneath; there is no other. (Deuteronomy 4:39)

Yours, O LORD, is the greatness and the power and the glory and the victory and the majesty, for all that is in the heavens and in the earth is yours. Yours is the kingdom, O LORD, and you are exalted as head above all. (1 Chronicles 29:11)

For the LORD, the Most High, is to be feared, a great king over all the earth. (Psalm 47:2)

17. May we make images or pictures of God to help us worship him?

No. God does not want us to make idols of any kind. No idol can begin to represent the eternal and invisible God or help us worship God in the way he wants us to worship him. Idols always lead people away from God and never draw them closer to him.

Scripture References
You shall not make for yourself a carved image, or any likeness of anything that is in heaven above, or that is in the earth beneath, or that is in the water under the earth. (Exodus 20:4)
Being then God's offspring, we ought not to think that the divine being is like gold or silver or stone, an image formed by the art and imagination of man. (Acts 17:29)

18. Is it possible for us to understand everything about God?

No. Though we are made in the image of God and in some ways are like God, God is a spiritual and eternal being who is far greater than we will ever be able to understand. We should therefore not reject or deny things which the Bible teaches us about God simply because they are beyond our human understanding.

Scripture References
Can you find out the deep things of God? Can you find out the limit of the Almighty? It is higher than heaven . . . Deeper than Sheol. . . . Its measure is longer than the earth and broader than the sea. (Job 11:7-9)
For as the heavens are higher than the earth, so are my ways higher than your ways and my thoughts than your thoughts. (Isaiah 55:9)
Oh the depth of the riches of the wisdom and knowledge of God! How unsearchable are his judgments, and how inscrutable his ways! "For who has known the mind of the Lord, or who has been his counselor?" "Or who has given a gift to him that he might be repaid?" For from him and through him and to him are all things. To him be glory forever. Amen. (Romans 11:33-36)

Exploring Further

1. What are some of the most important things we should believe about God?

Among the most important truths about God are the following: There is only one true God. This one God is eternal, all-knowing, everywhere present, spiritual, invisible, all-powerful, wise, patient, compassionate, loving, just, holy, and unchanging in his being. He exists as three persons whom the Bible reveals as the Father, the Son, and the Holy Spirit. These three persons together form the Holy Trinity. God created the world in the beginning as a perfect world which he himself said was "very good." He created a man and a woman in his own image and put them in charge of the earth and all creatures on the earth. He continues to maintain and sustain the world but will eventually judge all people who have ever lived. In his mercy he will grant everlasting life to all those who have repented of their sin and put their trust in Jesus Christ for salvation. In his justice, he will destroy those who refuse to repent and refuse to put their trust in God and his Son Jesus. He will then establish a new heaven and a new earth and will reign forever with his redeemed people who will live in perfect and never-ending joy and peace.

2. Can we fully understand everything the Bible teaches about God?

No. Because God is eternal, infinite, and Triune (three in one), there are many things we cannot fully understand about God or his ways. We should not expect to be able to understand everything about God with our human limitations and finite existence any more than animals can fully understand us as human beings. It is important, therefore, that we do not reject something which the Bible says simply because we cannot understand it or do not like it. If we reject something which the Bible clearly teaches, we are making ourselves judges of the Bible rather than submitting our limited knowledge and understanding to the eternal truth of God's holy Word. God's truth stands eternal and supreme whether or not we can understand all if it.

3. Why is it significant for us that there is only one true God?

If there were more gods than the one true God, each god would be extremely limited by the existence, power, and authority of the other gods. We would live in constant uncertainty concerning the power and authority of OUR god in relation to other gods. And we would probably often wonder if the gods were jealous of one another or in conflict with one another—as people are. If there actually were many gods, it would be impossible for us to love and serve each one with all our heart, soul, mind, and strength. Our loyalties would always be somewhat divided. And we could never find the peace and confidence and joy we now have in knowing and serving the one and only true God.

4. What would your life be like if there were no God?

If there were no true God, we would not exist at all. But just supposing we somehow existed and God did not, we would have to depend completely on ourselves or other human beings for everything. There would be no way to find genuine forgiveness, no sure hope for the future, no divine power to bless, encourage, comfort and strengthen us, no divine power to administer justice, and no one with divine love and compassion to be concerned about our present or future well-being. The ultimate power on earth would be found in the persons with the greatest wealth, prestige, or influence, and no one could contest their judgments, decisions, or actions. There might possibly be some earthly authorities or powers who would encourage people to act justly and compassionately, but their powers would be very limited and their influence would be very temporary. Relatively few powerful dictators in history have been genuinely kind and benevolent, and none of them has stayed in power for more than (at most) a few decades. If there is no righteous and powerful Judge, the evils of this world would never be set right, life would have little meaning, and mankind would have little enduring hope.

5. What would your life be like if there was a God but you did not know Him personally?

Regrettably, there are millions and millions of people who do not know the true God. Some of these people live reasonably comfortable lives as they focus on their earthly activities and do not even try to deal with guilt, sin, or moral failure and do not believe in or bother with the possibility of life after death. As far as they are concerned, this life is all there is. Some of those who believe this way do demonstrate a significant concern about others and seek to help them make the most of their earthly life. Others focus on getting everything they can for themselves without bothering at all about others. Whether they are kind or selfish, however, they miss the greatest blessings possible for us on this earth—knowing the love and mercy and grace of God. They totally cut themselves off from the incredible eternal blessings which are promised to those who know and love and trust God as he has revealed himself to us in the Bible and in his Son Jesus Christ.

6. Why is it wrong to make idols or images of God?

God has strongly and repeatedly commanded us in the Bible not to make images or idols of himself. There is no way in which any image or idol can even begin to meaningfully represent the eternal, almighty, infinite, compassionate Creator and Judge of our world. Every image or idol, no matter how big or artistic or expensive, would belittle and misrepresent God, the eternal Spirit. Besides, if someone was able to make a beautiful idol of some kind, many people would soon be worshiping the idol rather than the God which the idol supposedly represented. Throughout history people have been led astray by their idols and images. God has never been glorified or honored by any human effort to represent him with a physical image. As Jesus himself said: *"God is spirit, and those who worship him must worship in spirit and truth" (John 4:24).*

7. What are some of the things people can learn about God if they do not have a Bible or someone to teach them?

God has revealed himself in history through his work of creation, through miracles, through changing the lives of those who trusted in him, and through his divine intervention at various points throughout history. Even without the Bible or a teacher, people can know from the created world that God is real, mighty, wise, orderly, and glorious. They can know from the growth of crops, the taste of food, and the enjoyment of other pleasures that God is generous and delightful. They can know from their own conscience that God is righteous, because their conscience can sense that right and wrong are defined by Someone outside themselves. By seeing that all people die and that all governments eventually fail, they can see that God is just and punishes sinful humanity with death. They can know from hearing about miracles or observing transformed Christians that God is supernaturally active among people still today. (See Psalm 19:1-4, Romans 1:19, Acts 14:16-17 Deuteronomy 10:17-18; Psalm 4:1-3, Psalm 50:6, Psalm 89:5-8, Psalm 97:6, Psalm 104:1-31, Psalm 147:16-18, Psalm 148:6-13, Isaiah 6:3, Isaiah 40:21-26, Daniel 2:21, 46-47.) It's true, of course, that many people do not acknowledge God or praise him, even though they see God's handiwork in creation, or taste God's goodness in daily blessings, or sense God's righteousness through the voice of conscience, or observe God's just wrath in the reality of death. However, even when people suppress their knowledge of God, those who do so are without excuse, as Romans 1:19 says.

8. What can you learn about God from the Bible that you cannot learn in any other way?

The Bible teaches us many spiritual truths that cannot be taught through nature or natural events. For example, the Bible teaches us about the love and righteousness and holiness of God as well as other attributes of God. It also teaches us about right and wrong, obedience and disobedience, punishment, justice, forgiveness, compassion, hope, heaven and hell. The Bible clearly teaches us about Jesus, the way of salvation through

Christ alone, and the person and work of the Holy Spirit. The Bible also describes the kind of life that honors God and teaches us what displeases or dishonors him. In the Bible we read stories that encourage us, warn us, inform us, and enable us to better understand the ways of God in this world and in the lives of his people. The Bible teaches many other things that we do not learn just by observing nature or history—things about holiness, mercy, prayer, personal sacrifice, dedication, family, marriage, government, giving, witnessing, and other parts of daily life.

9. If you had only 20 minutes to teach someone about God, what are the things you would talk about?

Your answer may depend to some extent on a person's age, background, education, interests, and circumstances. However, there are certain basic or fundamental truths about God which are so important that every person, young or old, well-educated or uneducated, rich or poor, weak or strong, should know. Included would be such things as the fact that there is only one true God who is perfectly holy and just, the creator of the world, the divine and righteous judge of every person, and a God of mercy, forgiveness, and love. Everyone should also know that God sent his only begotten Son into the world to give his life as an atonement for our sin and to give us the joy and hope of eternal life with him in glory. Helpful Scripture verses would include such passages as John 4:24, 1 Timothy 6:15-16, Exodus 34:6-7 and John 3:16. The primary purpose of asking this question is to help you focus on some basic truths which you should be able to present to any person at any time without hesitation and with strong Biblical support.

10. What are some of the truths about God which are most important to you personally?

Think about this, meditate on God's awesome reality, and explore what truths of God have stirred your heart.

Lesson Three: Origins

Introduction

Many people wonder about the origin of our world. They ask: "Where did everything come from? How did the universe get started? Was there someone who made this beautiful and complex world? Or did everything just happen by chance?"

Today many people believe that everything in our world came about simply by chance. They teach that all that exists in the world came into being through a long, slow process of mindless evolution. There was no one to start the process and no one to guide it. Things just happened! Animals and people and flowers and trees and mountains and hills and everything that exists made their entrance into the world with no purpose and no future. But if that is true, then we human beings are also simply an accident with no real purpose in the present and no meaningful hope for the future. We live for a few years, we die, and we are forgotten.

But that's not what happened. Human beings didn't gradually make their appearance in the world without any purpose or direction. They were created by a powerful, loving, and eternal God. They were created as intelligent beings who had the potential of enjoying a wonderful and joyful life with other human beings and also with their Creator. God even created them in his own image, so they could know him and love him and serve him. God also gave them the privilege and the task of ruling over the rest of his beautiful creation so that everything would serve the purpose for which God created it. And if they continued to love and serve him, they would live forever in peace and joy and harmony with the God who created them.

However, the world today is obviously no longer a world of perfect harmony and unending delight. Beautiful flowers wilt and die. Streams and rivers overflow or dry up. Hurricanes, floods and storms bring terrible destruction. People get sick and die. Nation rises up against nation, and people hurt and kill one another. Tensions and strife abound. Misery is found everywhere.

Many people wonder why there are so many good and beautiful things in our world while, at the same time, there are also many things that are neither good nor beautiful. Did the world start out good and then become bad? Or did it start out bad and then gradually get better? Or were there both good and bad things from the very beginning?

In this lesson you will read the Bible's answers to those questions.

1. Where did our universe come from?

God created the entire universe out of nothing by his almighty power.

Scripture References
In the beginning, God created the heavens and the earth. (Genesis 1:1)
By faith we understand that the universe was created by the word of God, so that what is seen was not made out of things that are visible. (Hebrews 11:3)
[God] created heaven and what is in it, the earth and what is in it, and the sea and what is in it. (Revelation 10:6)

2. What was the earth like in the very beginning?

Before God formed the earth into a beautiful place for man to live, the earth was formless, dark and empty.

Scripture Reference
The earth was without form and void, and darkness was over the face of the deep. And the Spirit of God was hovering over the face of the waters. (Genesis 1:2)

3. Where did the sun and moon and stars and all the plants and animals come from?

Genesis 1 says repeatedly, "God said," and when God spoke, things came into being. Other passages in the Bible indicate that the world was fashioned by the "hands" of the Lord. All of these passages teach us that God was the Creator who used his divine power to bring into being a beautiful, wonderful, and incredible universe.

Scripture References
And God said, "Let there be light," and there was light. (Genesis 1:3)
Of old you [God] laid the foundation of the earth, and the heavens are the work of your hands. (Psalm 102:25)

4. Was the original creation good or bad or mixed?

The world that God created in the beginning was good in every way. After each act of creation recorded in Genesis 1, we read the specific words: "God saw that it was good." And, at the end of God's initial creative work, we read that everything God had made was "very good." Sin had not yet entered the world and the earth was free from corruption, disharmony and decay.

Scripture References
God saw that it was good. (Genesis 1:10, 12, 18, 21, 25)
And God saw everything that he had made, and, behold, it was very good. (Genesis 1:31)

5. Where did human beings come from?

After God had prepared the earth as a home for human beings, he made a man and a woman in his image and likeness to rule over his creation. Though the man was created before the woman, both man and woman were made in God's image and both had equal standing in the sight of God.

Scripture References
Then God said, "Let us make man in our image, after our likeness." . . . So God created man in his own image, in the image of God he created him; male and female he created them. And God blessed them. And God said to them, "Be fruitful and multiply and fill the earth and subdue it." (Genesis 1:26-28)

6. How did God create the first man and the first woman?

God first made a man from the dust of the ground and breathed into his nostrils the breath of life. Later, God took a rib from man's side and made a woman from the rib.

Scripture References
Then the LORD God formed the man of dust of the ground and breathed into his nostrils the breath of life, and the man became a living creature. (Genesis 2:7)
Then the LORD God said, "It is not good that the man should be alone; I will make him a helper fit for him." . . . So the LORD God caused a deep sleep to fall upon the man, and while he slept took one of his ribs and closed up its place with flesh. And the rib that the LORD God had taken from the man he made into a woman. (Genesis 2:18, 21, 22)

7. What were the names of the first man and the first woman?

The first man was called *Adam* (which may mean *ground* or *human being*). Adam named his wife *Eve* (which may mean *life-giver*).

Scripture Reference
The man called his wife's name Eve, because she was the mother of all living. (Genesis 3:20)

8. Where did Adam and Eve live?

God placed them in a beautiful garden called the Garden of Eden. No one knows exactly where this was, but it likely was somewhere in the part of the world we know as the Middle East.

Scripture Reference

And the LORD God planted a garden in Eden, in the east, and there he put the man whom he had formed. (Genesis 2:8)

9. What responsibilities did God give to Adam and Eve?

God told them to be fruitful, to fill the earth, to rule over it, and to take care of it. God provided them with everything necessary—mentally and physically—to do what he had commanded them to do.

Scripture Reference

God blessed them. And God said to them, "Be fruitful and multiply and fill the earth and subdue it and have dominion over the fish of the sea and over the birds of the heavens and over every living thing that moves on the earth." (Genesis 1:28)

10. What test did God give to Adam and Eve?

God told Adam and Eve that they might eat from every tree in the Garden of Eden where they were living except for one tree called "the tree of the knowledge of good and evil." God very clearly and very strongly commanded them not to eat of this one tree. This was to be a test of their love for God, their trust in God, and their obedience to God.

Scripture Reference

And the LORD God commanded the man, saying, "You may surely eat of every tree of the garden, but of the tree of the knowledge of good and evil you shall not eat, for in the day that you eat of it you shall surely die." (Genesis 2:16-17)

11. Did Adam and Eve obey God's command?

They did obey at first, but when Satan, an evil spirit, came to them in the form of a serpent, he lied to them, tempted them to eat from the tree, and promised them that if they did eat of it, they would become like God himself. They listened to Satan, believed him, and ate from the tree instead of obeying and trusting God.

Scripture References
Now the serpent was more crafty than any other beast of the field that the LORD God had made. He said to the woman, "Did God actually say, 'You shall not eat of any tree in the garden'?" (Genesis 3:1)
So when the woman saw that the tree was good for food, and that it was a delight to the eyes, and that the tree was to be desired to make one wise, she took of its fruit and ate, and she also gave some to her husband who was with her, and he ate. (Genesis 3:6)
. . . that ancient serpent called the devil, or Satan, who leads the whole world astray. (Revelation 12:9)

12. What was the result of their disobedience?

First of all, Adam and Eve immediately died spiritually. That is, they died in their relationship with God. Things were no longer the same between them and God. They lost their fellowship with God, they lost the joy they previously had in walking and talking with God, and they became afraid of God rather than delighting in being with him. They also became aware of their nakedness for the first time and felt ashamed in God's presence. Their disobedience also led eventually to their physical death. Further, the entire world was affected by their sin. There were still many good and beautiful things in the world after they sinned, but for the first time the world became subject to suffering, pain, decay, and death.

Scripture References
The man and his wife hid themselves from the presence of the LORD God among the trees of the garden. (Genesis 3:8)
To the woman he said, "I will surely multiply your pain in childbearing; in pain you shall bring forth children. Your desire shall be for your husband, and he shall rule over you." And to Adam he said, "Because you have listened to the voice of your wife and have eaten of the tree of which I commanded you, 'You

*shall not eat of it,' cursed is the ground because of you; in pain
you shall eat of it all the days of your life; thorns and thistles it
shall bring forth for you; and you shall eat the plants of the field.
By the sweat of your face you shall eat bread, till you return to
the ground, for out of it you were taken; for you are dust, and to
dust you shall return." (Genesis 3:16-19)*

13. What does the sin of Adam have to do with us today?

Adam was the representative of the entire human race. When
he sinned, everyone was affected by the consequences of his sin.
All of us now come into this world with a sinful human nature
which is inclined toward evil rather than toward good. The world
in which we live is a world filled with suffering, sorrow, pain,
decay and death. And no matter how strong and healthy we may
be, we know that our lives, too, will end in death. The results of
Adam's disobedience and sin are far greater and more significant
than Adam could ever have imagined when he gave in to
temptation and listened to Satan rather than to God.

Scripture References
*Sin came into the world through one man, and death through sin,
and so death spread to all men because all sinned. (Romans
5:12)
The whole creation has been groaning together in the pains of
childbirth until now. (Romans 8:22)
In Adam all die. (1 Corinthians 15:22)*

14. Does this mean that everyone in the whole world is guilty before God?

Yes. There are no exceptions except for Jesus Christ, who
was perfectly sinless and was not born with a sinful human
nature.

Scripture References
*None is righteous, no, not one. (Romans 3:10)
For all have sinned and fall short of the glory of God. (Romans
3:23)*

And in him [Jesus] is no sin. (1 John 3:5)

15. Won't a loving God simply overlook the fact that we are all sinners?

No. Though God is gracious and merciful, he is also holy and just. He cannot and will not let sin go unpunished.

Scripture References
The LORD is slow to anger and abounding in steadfast love, forgiving iniquity and transgression, but he will by no means clear the guilty. (Numbers 14:18)
The LORD is slow to anger and great in power, and the LORD will by no means clear the guilty. (Nahum 1:3)
Do not be deceived: God is not mocked, for whatever one sows, that will he also reap. (Galatians 6:7)

16. Since we are all sinners before God, is there no hope for any of us?

There certainly is hope! Even before God pronounced judgment on Adam and Eve for what they had done (*Genesis 3:16-19),* he said that he would eventually defeat the powers of evil and destroy them (*Genesis 3:15*). Thousands of years of human history passed, however, before Jesus came into our world to pay the penalty for Adam's sin and also for our own sins.

Scripture References
The LORD God said to the serpent [Satan], "I will put enmity between you and the woman, and between your offspring and her offspring; he shall bruise your head, and you shall bruise his heel." (Genesis 3:14-15)
As a father shows compassion to his children, so the LORD shows compassion to those who fear him. For he knows our frame; he remembers that we are dust. (Psalm 103:13-14)

Exploring Further

1. What difference would it make in your life if you did not believe that God created the world?

If God didn't create the world, then all of us are here simply by chance. We would have no real hope for the future and would definitely have no certainty of having eternal life with Christ. We would probably focus much more on meeting our own needs or desires and have less interest in helping to meet the needs of others. We might also throw off some restraints which presently keep us from doing things which we believe would bring dishonor to the name of God. We obviously would not gather with others for worship of the Creator and we would probably not spend much (or any) time reading and studying the Bible. Some of us might work hard to preserve the world and its resources, since that is all there is. However, others might have less concern for the natural world and would have little concern about trying to preserve it.

2. How important is it for us to know how old the earth is?

Some believers feel that it is very important to know (approximately) how old the world is because they believe that the Bible teaches that the earth is relatively young. Some of them are also convinced that science demonstrates that the world is not nearly as old as many people claim. Other believers, however, are not at all concerned about scientific teachings about the age of the earth. They strongly believe that the Bible does not intend to teach us anything about the age of the earth. Rather, they emphasize that the Bible clearly teaches that GOD has created the world but does not give us any definite indication of the time when he created it or the length of time it took him to create it. And they give some very thoughtful arguments to support their position.

Does it make any difference which position is correct? For many people it makes a lot of difference. For others it makes no difference at all. Clearly, the most important thing is to remember that "in the beginning GOD created the heavens and the earth"—no matter when that happened or how long it took.

It may also be helpful to remember that for many years believers emphasized that the earth was the center of the universe and that the sun rotated around the earth. Those who believed and taught this based their argument—at least partly—on their understanding of the Bible. Very few today, however, believe that or teach that any longer. And few people seem to be disturbed about the fact that the sun only appears to rise and set—even though the Bible uses language which might seem to indicate that it actually does rise and set. Even today, knowing that the earth moves around the sun, we still speak of sunrise and sunset. It's important for us not to insist that the Bible teaches something which it does not intend to teach. On the other hand, it's also important to recognize that the scientific community has also changed its position on a number of things over the years, so we should not accept everything taught by scientists as ultimate truth.

The Bible is clearly our final authority on matters of faith and doctrine and Christian living, but we should not claim that the Bible teaches something it does not intend to teach.

3. How important is it to know exactly how God created the world and how long it took to create it?

Many Christians strongly believe that God created the world in six ordinary days of twenty-four hours each. They argue that the first chapter of Genesis and Exodus 20:11 allow no other interpretation. Any evolution that did take place (such as micro-evolution involved in the formation of new species), took place after the original creation described in Genesis.

Other Christians believe that God brought our world and various life forms into existence through a long, gradual process called macro-evolution. Though the process may have been very slow, they believe that God was in complete control of all that took place.

It is very important to remember that this disagreement among Christians is not about the WHO of creation but the HOW of creation. Those who believe that God simply spoke the world into existence do not believe that the formation of the world took a long time. Those who believe that God brought the world into being over a long period of time do not believe that the work of creation was limited to just six days. Both groups, however, agree that this is our Father's world and recognize that God was the One who brought our complex world into existence. He also is the One we must recognize and honor as the creator and sustainer of our world and the One who will determine the world's future as well as its beginning.

Without going into great detail, it is helpful to recognize some of the reasons why some Christians believe that Genesis 1 is not intended to present a literal description of the creation of the world. One may accept or reject these reasons, but it is at least helpful to be aware of them. Among the reasons are the following.

a. The account in Genesis 1 is significantly different in several ways from that in Genesis 2. Some argue, therefore, that it is quite possible that neither chapter *intends* to give us details of the time or method of the creation of the world.

b. Genesis 1 gives us the impression that God spoke and suddenly all kinds of creative activity took place. Other passages, however, refer to the hand or arm or fingers of God in creating the world. (See, for example, Psalm 8:3, 6; Psalm 19:1; Psalm 102:25; Isaiah 45:12; Zechariah 12:1; Hebrews 1:10.) Both the Genesis account and the other passages may be speaking poetically without intending to give us details of the method God used to bring the world into existence.

c. Genesis 1 indicates that the earth brought forth vegetation (Genesis 1:11-13) and also brought forth the animal world (Genesis 1:24-25). We all recognize that plants and trees grow out of the ground but we also know that animals are normally produced by a totally different process. Does Genesis 1:24-25 intend to teach us that the land produced both vegetation and animals? (Some believers did seem to teach that in the past and some may still do so today.)

d. Genesis 1:14-19 describes the creation of the sun and moon in some detail but provides only a very brief reference to the creation of the rest of the starry world. We realize today that the earth with its sun and moon form only a very tiny fraction of the entire universe, but Genesis 1 gives us little information concerning the creation of most of the universe.

e. Genesis 1:16-27 refers to the creation of Adam and Eve on the 6th day after the creation of the animal world on that day. However, Genesis 2:19-22 indicates that Eve was apparently created some time later after Adam became painfully aware that he did not have a "partner" as the animals did.

f. Genesis 1:1-2 seems to describe the "original" creation as a world that was dark and formless and empty. Many regard that as an unusual beginning for the creation of a perfect earth! Moreover, since there is no indication how much time existed between verse 2 and verse 3 in Genesis 1, some believe that verse 2 may possibly describe an earlier world which might have been destroyed and then re-created in some way. Some suggest that this earlier earth might have been inhabited by angels (or other beings) who were created by God but then later fell into disobedience and sin which led to the destruction of their world. There is obviously no definite proof of this, but we do know that the angelic world was created before the human world and Satan fell into sin before Adam and Eve were created. The first three verses of Genesis do therefore seem to provide room for various interpretations of the creation account.

g. Genesis 1 is written in a poetic form which has a unique structure not found in Genesis 2. Since most people recognize that poetry in the Bible (such as that found in the books of Psalms and Proverbs) is often not interpreted literally, some people argue that Genesis 1 should not be interpreted literally either.

These are some of the reasons why some Christians teach that the account of Genesis 1:2-31 is not intended to represent a complete or literal account of God's work of creation in the beginning. One may reject those arguments, but it is helpful to be aware of them when making judgments concerning the manner and length of the creation process.

4. Since God told Adam and Eve to rule over the earth and all he had made, what are some of the implications of that for our lives today?

It is important for Christians to promote those activities which make the best possible use of the earth's resources. We should not disregard or take lightly any activities which unnecessarily spoil the earth or waste any of its resources. Neither should we carelessly pollute the atmosphere or our streams, lakes, and rivers. We should also protect the animal world from careless and thoughtless destruction. Though believers value the spiritual dimensions of life over the material ones, we recognize that we have to make the best possible use of all that the Lord has entrusted to us. Christians should not thoughtlessly use the earth's resources in order to promote the economic well-being of a few while neglecting the fact that others may be hurt in some way by what they are doing.

God is not glorified when we treat his world in a way which does not honor him as the Creator and sustainer of the universe he has made. Though the earth will someday be destroyed by fire according to God's eternal plan (2 Peter 3:10-12), this does not give us the right to treat God's creation without appropriate care and concern.

5. What are some of the practical implications of the fact that God created man and woman in his image?

In some parts of the world women are still regarded as "second class citizens." They are considered to be less important, less valuable, and less worthy than men and are treated accordingly. They do not have the same rights or privileges that men have and often do not have equal standing with men in a court of law. In marriage they may be considered important only for giving birth to children—especially male children. Their husbands may have other wives or mistresses if they so choose and wives may be considered disposable when their husbands tire of them. Even some Christians (hopefully not many), may be so strongly influenced by their culture and upbringing that they may try to justify their belief and/or feeling that women truly are inferior to men.

All of these things, however, are totally wrong and in conflict with the Bible's teaching that men and women are both image bearers of God and should be treated accordingly. Women should be treated with respect and honor and should be given equal privileges in society and before the law. Though the Bible teaches that men should have a leadership position in marriage, this does not mean that women are less valuable or less important than men. (This subject will be discussed at greater length in Lesson Nine.)

6. In what way did Adam and Eve "die" when they disobeyed God?

When Adam and Eve sinned, their bodies became subject to physical death and they lost the relationship of love, trust, and obedience between themselves and God which they had once enjoyed. Unless something miraculous would happen in their lives, their bodies would eventually die and they would live apart from God forever. Their hearts were no longer in tune with God, and their goals and desires were no longer God-centered. They were destined to live in a world that was cursed by God—a life of pain, suffering, and toilsome labor where physical death became the destiny of all living creatures.

That does not mean that there would never be any joy or pleasure for them on earth, but they were separated from the beautiful, holy, and pure life which they had enjoyed before they sinned. Ephesians 2:1-3 describes their situation (and the situation of all people who are apart from Christ) in the following words: *And you were dead in the trespasses and sins in which you once walked, following the course of this world, following the prince of the power of the air, the spirit that is now at work in the sons of disobedience—among whom we all once lived in the passions of our flesh, carrying out the desires of the body and the mind, and were by nature children of wrath, like the rest of mankind.* Romans 5:10 describes unbelievers as *"enemies of God"* and Colossians 1:21 refers to them as people who are *"alienated"* from God.

It's important to remember, however, that God in his mercy continues to shower many blessings upon both believers and unbelievers, on those who are just and those who are not (Matthew 5:45, Acts 14:15-17). Many people are still able to enjoy times of pleasure and plenty, even though they are not worthy of these blessings and do not thank God for them. However, earthly life is often filled with sorrow and sickness, frustration and disappointment, and eventually everyone will stand before God in judgment. And then, for those who are not in Christ, the time of joy and gladness will be completely gone forever.

7. **Since God is gracious and forgiving, why should we be concerned about obeying him?**

God is truly loving and gracious and is willing to forgive us when we sincerely repent of doing wrong. However, he is also a holy God who commands us to love him with all our heart, soul, mind and strength. If we live carelessly or seek first of all to fulfill our own desires rather than loving and serving God, we obviously do not love God the way we should. All sin grieves God and dishonors him. If we don't remember that or fail to live in the light of that truth, we are putting ourselves ahead of God. If we sin carelessly and thoughtlessly, we also lose the effectiveness of any witness we may try to give to others concerning God and his salvation. As has often been stated, "Actions speak louder than words." If we talk to others about the power and majesty and greatness of God but do not love and serve him with all our heart, our words will have very little effect and the Lord will certainly not be honored or praised.

Also, we should never forget that we must someday give an account to God of all that we think, say, or do. Those who seek to live holy and honorable lives will graciously be rewarded by a loving and merciful God. Those who profess Christ but do not live holy and honorable lives will lose the rewards they might have received.

8. **In what way did Adam's sin affect us?**

According to Romans 5:12-18, Adam was our representative and the head of the entire human race. So, when Adam sinned, everyone sinned in him. All people who ever lived (except Jesus) were "in" Adam and all are affected by what he did. Romans 5:12 says: *Sin came into the world through one man, and death through sin, and so death spread to all men because all sinned.* And in Romans 5:19 we read: *By the one man's disobedience the many were made sinners.* Because Adam was the father of us all, we are all born with a sinful human nature (Psalm 51:5) and are therefore considered *dead in our trespasses* (Ephesians 2:5). Because of Adam's sin, the entire world of nature was also negatively affected (Genesis 3:17-19), so we all now live in a world that is under the curse of God. There are still many good and beautiful and pleasant things in our world, but it is far from what it was in the beginning.

9. In what way was Adam like Jesus?

Adam was the representative of every one of his descendants. Because of his sin, we are all considered guilty before God and are born with a sinful human nature. Jesus became the new representative of all who trust him and believe in him. Jesus did what none of us could ever do for ourselves. He paid the penalty for our sins and promised that all who trust and believe in him will have the gift of eternal life! Romans 5:15-18 teaches us: *For if many died through one man's trespass, much more have the grace of God and the free gift by the grace of that one man Jesus Christ abounded for many. . . For if, because of one man's trespass, death reigned through that one man, much more will those who receive the abundance of grace and the free gift of righteousness reign in life through the one man Jesus Christ. Therefore, as one trespass led to condemnation for all men, so one act of righteousness leads to justification and life for all men.*

10. What does the Bible means when it says in 2 Corinthians 4:4 that Satan is the "god of this world"?

God continues to rule over the entire world and has given all power and authority in heaven and on earth to his eternal Son, Jesus Christ. According to Ephesians 1:18-22, Jesus reigns *far above all rule and authority and power and dominion, and above every name that is named, not only in this age but also in the one to come. And he put all things under his feet and gave him as head over all things to the church.* See also Matthew 28:18 where Jesus is quoted as saying, *"All authority in heaven and on earth has been given to me."*

However, when Satan tempted Adam and Eve to disobey God, Satan gained a position of great authority and power in this world. Sin put humans in league with Satan and trapped them in the grip of his authority. Satan is a powerful opponent of both God and man and continues to tempt people to follow himself rather than Jesus. See, for example, 1 Peter 5:8: *Your adversary the devil prowls around like a roaring lion, seeking someone to devour.* Because Satan has this power, he is called "the god of this world." It is very important to remember, however, that Satan is not the "god" over those who belong to Jesus. Besides, even though his power is great, it is also very limited. Any authority he claims is usurped and not rightfully his. Satan can do nothing to God's people without the permission of the real ruler of the universe, our Lord Jesus Christ. See, for example, Luke 22:31 where Satan had to ask Jesus for permission to tempt and ruin Simon Peter. Also see the story of Job where Satan could do nothing against Job or his family without God's permission. (Job 1:6 through Job 2:10).

See also the comforting and encouraging words of 1 John 4:4,15-16: *"He who is in you is greater than he who is in the world. . . . Whoever confesses that Jesus is the Son of God, God abides in him and he in God. So we have come to know and to believe the love that God has for us."* We should never underestimate the power of Satan, but we should not overestimate it either. Satan is powerful compared to humans but not compared to God.

Lesson Four: Jesus Christ

Introduction

When Adam and Eve sinned in the Garden of Eden, they became afraid and tried to hide from God. They knew they had disobeyed God and felt ashamed. They no longer wanted to have God in their lives. But God, in his love, sought them out and talked with them.

God told them that they would surely be punished for their disobedience. But he also brought them a message of hope. He assured them that suffering and pain and death would not have the last word in their lives. They would not have to live forever in despair! Someday, God said, the evil one (Satan) who had deceived them would be completely crushed and destroyed. Satan would not have the final victory. God would!

The person who would accomplish this great victory was Jesus Christ. Jesus would not only destroy Satan, but he would also bring forgiveness and peace and would restore people to a loving and joyful relationship with God. Adam and Eve did not understand all of this, but God knew exactly what he was going to do in the future.

In this lesson you will learn more about this wonderful person we know as Jesus.

1. Who is Jesus?

Jesus is the eternal Son of God who came to earth as a human being. Before his birth, he existed from eternity as the "Word of God" through whom the world was created. As God's beloved eternal Son, Jesus is one of the three divine persons of the Holy Trinity, along with the Father and the Holy Spirit.

Scripture References
In the beginning was the Word, and the Word was with God, and the Word was God. . . . All things were made through him, and

54

without him was not anything made that was made. . . . The Word became flesh and dwelt among us. (John 1:1, 3, 14)

By him all things were created, in heaven and on earth, visible and invisible . . . all things were created through him and for him. And he is before all things, and in him all things hold together. (Colossians 1:16-17)

In these last days he [God] has spoken to us by his Son, whom he appointed the heir of all things, through whom also he created the world. He is the radiance of the glory of God and the exact imprint of his nature, and he upholds the universe by the word of his power. (Hebrews 1:2-3)

The heavens were opened to him [Jesus], and he saw the Spirit of God descending like a dove and coming to rest on him; and behold, a voice from heaven said, "This is my beloved Son, with whom I am well pleased." (Matthew 3:16-17)

2. What else does the Bible tell us about Jesus?

Jesus willingly humbled himself and left his position in heavenly glory so that he could come to earth as a servant and give his life for the salvation of human beings. He did not seek to hold on to his position in heaven but freely laid it aside so that sinful human beings might find forgiveness for their sins and live with him forever in glory.

Scripture References

Christ Jesus, who though he was in the form of God . . . made himself nothing, taking the form of a servant, being born in the likeness of men. And being found in human form, he humbled himself by becoming obedient to the point of death, even death on a cross. (Philippians 2:6-8)

Jesus said: *"[Father] I glorified you on earth, having accomplished the work that you gave me to do. And now, Father, glorify me in your presence with the glory I had with you before the world existed." (John 17:4-5)*

3. How did Jesus come into our world?

Jesus was born as a human baby to a Jewish virgin named

Mary as the prophet Isaiah had prophesied hundreds of years earlier.

Scripture References

The virgin shall conceive and bear a son, and shall call his name Immanuel. (Isaiah 7:14)

For to us a child is born, to us a son is given; and the government shall be upon his shoulder, and his name shall be called Wonderful Counselor, Mighty God, Everlasting Father, Prince of Peace. Of the increase of his government and of peace there will be no end. (Isaiah 9:6-7)

Now the birth of Jesus Christ took place in this way. When his mother Mary had been betrothed to Joseph, before they came together she was found to be with child from the Holy Spirit. . . . All this took place to fulfill what the Lord had spoken by the prophet: "Behold, the virgin shall conceive and bear a son, and they shall call his name Immanuel" (which means, God with us). (Matthew 1:18-23)

The angel Gabriel was sent from God . . . to a virgin betrothed to a man whose name was Joseph. . . . And the virgin's name was Mary. And he came to her and said, ". . . You will conceive in your womb and bear a son, and you shall call his name Jesus. He will be great and will be called the Son of the Most High . . . and of his kingdom there will be no end." (Luke 1:26-33)

4. How was it possible for Mary to have a child as a virgin?

Mary conceived her child through the miraculous power of the Holy Spirit. Both Mary and her fiancé Joseph were totally surprised by the message of the angel who told them what was going to happen, but in humility and faith they accepted and believed what the angel had told them.

Scripture References

Mary said to the angel, "How will this be, since I am a virgin?" And the angel answered her, "The Holy Spirit will come upon you, and the power of the Most High will overshadow you; therefore the child to be born will be called holy—the son of God." (Luke 1:34-35)

An angel of the Lord appeared to him [Joseph] in a dream, saying, "Joseph son of David, do not fear to take Mary as your wife, for that which is conceived in her is from the Holy Spirit." (Matthew 1:20)

5. Where was Jesus born?

Jesus was born in a small town called Bethlehem, a few miles from Jerusalem, in the land of Israel. Because there was no room in the Bethlehem inn when Joseph and Mary came to the city from their home in Nazareth, Jesus was born in a cattle stall. By being born in Bethlehem, Jesus fulfilled another Old Testament prophecy made several hundred years earlier by the prophet Micah.

Scripture Reference
But you, O Bethlehem . . . from you shall come forth for me one who is to be ruler in Israel, whose coming forth is from of old, from ancient days. (Micah 5:2)
Joseph also went up from Galilee, from the town of Nazareth, to Judea, to the city of David, which is called Bethlehem, because he was of the house and lineage of David, to be registered with Mary, his betrothed, who was with child. And while they were there, the time came for her to give birth. (Luke 2:4-6)
In the Bible, read the story of Jesus' birth in Matthew 1:18-25 and Luke 2:1-20.

6. Why was he given the name *Jesus*?

Jesus was given his personal name because the name *Jesus* means *Savior* or *God Saves*. Mary and Joseph did not choose this name themselves. The name was given to them by the angel who told them about the child who was going to be born to Mary. The baby would be called *Jesus* because he would save his people from their sins.

Scripture References
The angel said to Joseph, *"She [Mary] will bear a son, and you*

shall call his name Jesus, for he will save his people from their sins." (Matthew 1:21)
Christ Jesus came into the world to save sinners. (1 Timothy 1:15)

7. Why is Jesus sometimes called "Christ" or "the Christ"?

Christ was originally more of a *title* than a personal name. The word *Christ* means "the anointed one." It has the same meaning as the word *Messiah* in the Old Testament. In Old Testament times, a person was chosen by God for a special role such as a prophet, a priest or a king and was then anointed with oil in a special ceremony. Jesus was the Messiah (the Christ) promised in the Old Testament. He was anointed by the Holy Spirit as the greatest Prophet, our only High Priest and our eternal King.

Both in the New Testament and in church history we therefore read about Jesus, Jesus Christ, Christ or Christ Jesus. Each of these names is appropriate, and many people use one name or the other without giving specific thought to the meaning of each name. Other believers, however, are very careful to use one name rather than another, depending on the specific context in which the name is used.

Scripture References
Someone once said to Jesus, *"I know that Messiah is coming (he who is called Christ). When he comes, he will tell us all things." Jesus said to her, "I who speak to you am he." (John 4:25-26)*
Jesus asked his disciples, *"Who do you say that I am?"* Simon Peter replied, *"You are the Christ, the Son of the living God." (Matthew 16:15-16)*
Martha said to Jesus, *"Yes, Lord; I believe that you are the Christ, the Son of God, who is coming into the world." (John 11:27)*

8. Was Jesus truly as human as we are?

Yes. Jesus had a human nature that was just like ours—except that he was perfectly sinless. Because he was truly human, Jesus was sometimes thirsty, hungry, tired, and in need of sleep. He could also be tempted by Satan (see Matthew 4:1-11). Because he was human, he not only could pay the penalty for our sins, but he can also understand our limitations, sympathize with our weaknesses, and understand when we fall. He also knows and understands our need for guidance, instruction, encouragement, comfort, and rest. He truly is a perfect Savior.

Scripture References

He [Jesus] had to be made like his brothers in every respect, so that he might make propitiation for the sins of the people. (Hebrews 2:17)

Jesus the Son of God . . . in every respect has been tempted as we are, yet without sin. (Hebrews 4:14-15)

He committed no sin, neither was deceit found in his mouth. When he was reviled, he did not revile in return; when he suffered, he did not threaten, but continued entrusting himself to him who judges justly. (1 Peter 2:22-23)

9. What did Jesus do while he was on the earth?

The Bible tells us very little about the first thirty years of Jesus' life. During most of that time, he apparently lived with his parents and brothers and sisters in the city of Nazareth. Around the age of thirty, he began his public ministry, going through the towns of Israel, teaching and preaching, healing the sick, casting out demons, forgiving sins, raising the dead, and helping those who were in need.

Scripture References

Jesus went throughout all the cities and villages, teaching in their synagogues and proclaiming the gospel of the kingdom and healing every disease and every affliction. (Matthew 9:35)

The blind receive their sight and the lame walk, lepers are cleansed and the deaf hear, and the dead are raised up, and the poor have good news preached to them. (Matthew 11:5)

Demons also came out of many, crying, "You are the Son of God!" (Luke 4:41)

To a notorious sinner who repented Jesus said, *"Your sins are forgiven." (Luke 7:48)*

10. How did the people respond to the miracles and teachings of Jesus?

Many of the people were amazed. Some of them knew about Jesus' family and wondered where he acquired his knowledge and his abilities. Others gladly followed him because of his powerful teaching and the wonderful miracles he performed. Many of the leaders opposed Jesus' teaching and accused him of breaking traditional Jewish laws. However, large numbers of the common people, as well as some leaders, came to believe in him.

Scripture References
They were astonished beyond measure, saying, "He has done all things well." (Mark 7:37)
Now when he [Jesus] was in Jerusalem at the Passover Feast, many believed in his name when they saw the signs that he was doing. (John 2:23)
Many even of the authorities believed in him, but for fear of the Pharisees they did not confess it, so that they would not be put out of the synagogue. (John 12:42)
(For more extensive accounts of the life of Jesus, read Matthew, Mark, Luke, and John in the New Testament.)

11. Did everyone who saw Jesus' miracles or who heard Jesus' teachings believe in him?

No. Many of the Jewish leaders were jealous of Jesus and rejected him and his teachings. They knew about Jesus' family and would not believe that Jesus had truly come down from heaven. They were especially upset by Jesus' claim that he truly was the Son of God. Eventually they handed him over to Pontius Pilate, the Roman governor, to be put to death.

Scripture References
They said, "Is not this Jesus, the son of Joseph, whose father and mother we know? How does he now say, 'I came down from

heaven'?" (John 6:42)
The high priest stood up and said [to Jesus]. .. "I adjure you by the living God, tell us if you are the Christ, the Son of God." Jesus said to him, "You have said so." (Matthew 26:62-64)
[Pilate] knew it was out of envy that they had delivered him [Jesus] up. (Matthew 27:18)

12. Did either the Jews or the Roman governor find any good reason to judge Jesus worthy of death?

No! The Jewish leaders tried hard to find reasons why Jesus should be put to death, but they couldn't find any. Pilate, the Roman governor, also personally examined Jesus. After the examination, Pilate publicly announced that he found Jesus to be innocent of any wrongdoing.

Scripture References
The chief priests and the whole Council were seeking false evidence against Jesus that they might put him to death, but they found none, though many false witnesses came forward. (Matthew 26:59-60)
Pilate went out again and said to them [the Jews gathered there], "See, I am bringing him [Jesus] out to you that you may know that I find no guilt in him." (John 19:4)

13. Why did Pilate finally decide to put Jesus to death even though he knew Jesus was innocent?

Jesus claimed to be the (spiritual) King of the Jews. The Jewish leaders persuaded Pilate that he would get into deep trouble with the Roman emperor if he let someone go free who claimed to be a king. The Jewish leaders made such an uproar that Pilate finally gave in to their demands and selfishly gave up on making a just decision.

Scripture References
Pilate sought to release him [Jesus], but the Jews cried out, "If you release this man, you are not Caesar's friend. Everyone who makes himself a king opposes Caesar." (John 19:12)

So when Pilate saw that he was gaining nothing, but rather that a riot was beginning, he took water and washed his hands before the crowd, saying, "I am innocent of this man's blood; see to it yourselves." (Matthew 27:24)

14. How did Jesus die?

The Roman soldiers mocked Jesus, spit on him, beat him, put a crown of thorns on his head, and then led him away to a place called Golgotha where he was nailed to a wooden cross.

Scripture References
Then the soldiers of the governor took Jesus . . . and they gathered the whole battalion before him. And they stripped him and put a scarlet robe on him, and twisting together a crown of thorns, they put it on his head and put a reed in his right hand. And kneeling before him, they mocked him, saying, "Hail, King of the Jews!" And they spit on him and took the reed and struck him on the head. And when they had mocked him, they stripped him of the robe and put his own clothes on him and led him away to crucify him. (Matthew 27:27-31)
And over his head they put the charge against him, which read, "This is Jesus, the King of the Jews." (Matthew 27:37)
It was now about the sixth hour, and there was darkness over the whole land until the ninth hour, while the sun's light failed. And the curtain of the temple was torn in two. Then Jesus, calling out with a loud voice, said, "Father, into your hands I commit my spirit!" And having said this he breathed his last. (Luke 23:44-46)

15. What happened to Jesus' body after he died?

Joseph, a secret follower of Jesus and a prominent member of the highest Jewish Council, received permission from Pilate to take Jesus' body down from the cross. He and a man named Nicodemus lovingly wrapped the body in a linen cloth, placed it in Joseph's own new tomb, and rolled a big stone in front of the tomb.

Scripture References

*Joseph of Arimathea, who was a disciple of Jesus, but secretly for
fear of the Jews, asked Pilate that he might take away the body of
Jesus, and Pilate gave him permission. So he came and took
away his body. Nicodemus also, who earlier had come to Jesus
by night, came bringing a mixture of myrrh and aloes . . . So they
took the body of Jesus and bound it in linen cloths with the
spices. (John 19:38-39)*
*Joseph took the body and wrapped it in a clean linen shroud and
laid it in his own new tomb, which he had cut in the rock. And he
rolled a great stone to the entrance of the tomb and went away.
(Matthew 27:59-60)*

16. Did Jesus' body stay in the grave?

No! After three days Jesus arose from the dead and came out
of the tomb in which he had been placed by Joseph and
Nicodemus. A violent earthquake took place and an angel came
down from heaven, rolled away the stone which had been in front
of Jesus' tomb, and sat on it. When some of Jesus' followers
came to the tomb to anoint the body of Jesus, they saw that the
stone was rolled away, the tomb was empty, and an angel was
there to tell them what had happened. (Note: The angel did not
roll away the stone so that Jesus could get out. He rolled away
the stone so that others could see that the tomb was empty.)

Scripture References

*Now after the Sabbath, toward the dawn of the first day of the
week, Mary Magdalene and the other Mary went to see the tomb.
And behold, there was a great earthquake, for an angel of the
Lord descended from heaven and came and rolled back the stone
and sat on it. His appearance was like lightning, and his clothing
white as snow. And for fear of him the guards trembled and
became like dead men. But the angel said to the women, "Do not
be afraid, for I know that you seek Jesus who was crucified. He is
not here, for he has risen, as he said." (Matthew 28:1-6)*
*God raised him up, loosing the pangs of death, because it was
not possible for him to be held by it. (Acts 2:24)*
Christ died for our sins . . . was buried . . . was raised on the

third day . . . Then he appeared to more than five hundred brothers at one time. (1 Corinthians 15:3-6)
(If you have a Bible, read the story of Jesus' crucifixion and resurrection in Matthew 27 and 28, Mark 15 and 16, Luke 23 and 24, and John 19 and 20.)

17. If Jesus was sinless, why did he have to die?

Jesus died in *our* place. He took on himself the punishment that *we* deserved. Only Jesus, the perfect and sinless Son of God, could pay the penalty for the sins of others. God the Father, out of love for us, directed his Son to die in order to save sinners. Jesus obeyed his Father in order to glorify God and save us. In his incredible love and grace, Jesus willingly gave his life so that we who put our trust in him will have eternal life in his glorious presence.

Scripture References
Jesus said, *"I lay down my life for the sheep. . . . No one takes it from me, but I lay it down of my own accord." (John 10:14,18)*
The night before he died, Jesus said, *"I do as the Father has commanded me, so that the world may know that I love the Father." (John 14:31)*
The wages of sin is death, but the free gift of God is eternal life in Christ Jesus our Lord. (Romans 6:23)
God shows his love for us in that while we were still sinners, Christ died for us. (Romans 5:8)
This is love: not that we have loved God but that he loved us and sent his Son to be the propitiation for our sins. (1 John 4:10)
For God so loved the world that he gave his only Son, that whoever believes in him should not perish but have eternal life. (John 3:16)

18. What did Jesus do after he arose from the grave?

For forty days he stayed on earth to prove to his followers that he was truly alive and also to give them further instructions. During those forty days he appeared to his disciples on various occasions and also to more than five hundred others at the same time.

Scripture References
He [Jesus] presented himself alive to them [his disciples] after his suffering by many proofs, appearing to them during forty days and speaking about the kingdom of God. (Acts 1:3)
He appeared to more than five hundred brothers at one time. (1 Corinthians 15:6)
Jesus came and said to them [his disciples], "All authority in heaven and on earth has been given to me. Go therefore and make disciples of all nations, baptizing them in the name of the Father and of the Son and of the Holy Spirit, teaching them to observe all that I have commanded you. And behold, I am with you always, to the end of the age." (Matthew 28:18-20)

19. What did Jesus do after the forty days?

Jesus returned to heaven where he now rules over all things in heaven and on earth.

Scripture References
So then the Lord Jesus, after he had spoken to them [his disciples], was taken up into heaven and sat down at the right hand of God. (Mark 16:19)
While he [Jesus] blessed them [his disciples], he parted from them and was carried up into heaven. (Luke 24:51)
[God] raised [Jesus] from the dead and seated him at his right hand in the heavenly places, far above all rule and authority and power and dominion, and above every name that is named, not only in this age but also in the one to come. And he [God] put all things under his [Jesus'] feet and gave him as head over all things to the church. (Ephesians 1:20-22)

20. Is Jesus ever going to come back to earth again?

Yes! Someday Jesus will return to earth and will gather all believers to live with him forever.

Scripture References
Jesus said, "In my Father's house are many rooms. If it were not so, would I have told you that I go to prepare a place for you? And if I go and prepare a place for you, I will come again and will take you to myself, that where I am you may be also." (John 14:2-3)

And while they [the disciples] were gazing into heaven as he [Jesus] went, behold, two men stood by them in white robes, and said, ". . . This Jesus, who was taken up from you into heaven, will come in the same way as you saw him go into heaven." (Acts 1:10-11)

Exploring Further

1. What did God promise in Genesis 3:15? Did Adam and Eve understand what God promised them?

God promised that he would put enmity between the woman (Eve) and her offspring and the serpent (Satan) and his offspring. There would be continual strife between Satan and his allies and all the descendants of Eve throughout human history. However, Eve's descendants would not live forever in separation from God and his blessing. Satan would not be victorious forever. One specific person, a descendant of Eve, would someday crush the head of the serpent, destroying his power. This person was Jesus Christ, God's eternal Son. Jesus would someday make provision for Adam and Eve's descendants to again live happily and joyfully with the God whom they had disobeyed.

However, though Satan would be crushed (defeated, destroyed), he would also cause much harm to the woman's descendants and would bring pain and suffering and even death to Jesus himself. The "heel" of the woman's seed would be "struck" by Satan, but Jesus and His followers would be eternally victorious.

Adam and Eve would not have understood all of this. The full meaning and significance of the promise of Genesis 3:15 would not be understood at any time before the coming of Jesus. However, the promise was there to give hope to everyone who trusted the Word of God in spite of all kinds of trials and fears and uncertainties in their lives.

Other passages in the Bible teach some of the same truths found in Genesis 3:15.

Revelation 12:1-17 gives a special picture of the birth of Jesus and the tremendous conflict that followed. Verse 17 reads: *"Then the dragon became furious with the woman and went off to make war on the rest of her offspring, on those who keep the commandments of God and hold to the testimony of Jesus."* The following chapters in the book of Revelation clearly indicate that Jesus and those who believe in him will be eternally victorious.

> *The God of peace will soon crush Satan under your feet. (Romans 16:20)*
> *Since therefore the children [human beings] share in flesh and blood, he himself (Jesus) likewise partook of the same things, that through death he might destroy the one who has the power of death, that is, the devil, and deliver all those who through fear of death were subject to lifelong slavery. (*Hebrews 2:14)
> *The devil has been sinning from the beginning. The reason the Son of God appeared was to destroy the works of the devil. (*1 John 3:8)

2. What do John 1:1-3 and Colossians 1:16-17 teach us about Jesus?

These passages clearly teach us that Jesus Christ was truly God in the flesh. Jesus is called the WORD of God who was *with* God and *was* God. Jesus was also the creator of our world.

Nothing was made without him. All things were made *for* him as well as *by* him. He is *before all things* and he is the One in whom the entire world *holds together* (Colossians 1:17).

These verses are among the strongest and clearest statements in the Bible that Jesus was and is truly God. Though Jesus himself was visible with a human body, he is called the *image of the invisible God, the firstborn over all creation*—that is, the One with authority and prestige and honor (Colossians 1:15). Some cults teach that John 1:1 teaches that Jesus was "a god" rather than GOD in the flesh. However, the original Greek of this passage does not support this heresy. Moreover, if Jesus was simply "a god" who is to be worshiped and honored alongside of the one true God, then the Bible would repeatedly contradict itself since it teaches us in many places that there is only one true God who is worthy of worship and praise. John 1:14 teaches: *The Word became flesh and dwelt among us, and we have seen his glory, glory as of the only Son from the Father, full of grace and truth.* And in John 1:18 we read: *No one has ever seen God; the only God, who is at the Father's side, he has made him known.*

Other passages confirm this same truth about the deity of Christ. For example, in Titus 2:13 we read of *our blessed hope, the appearing of the glory of our great God and Savior Jesus Christ.* 2 Peter 1:1 speaks of *the righteousness of our God and Savior Jesus Christ.* Paul teaches in Philippians 2:6 that before coming to earth as a human, Jesus was *in the form of God.* Revelation 1:17 describes Jesus as *the first and the last* and Revelation 21:6 and 22:13 refer to him as *the Alpha and the Omega* (titles also applied to God; see Revelation 1:8). Isaiah 9:6 refers to the coming Messiah (Jesus) as *Mighty God.* These exact same words are used in Isaiah 10:21 to refer to the only true God.

3. What does the Bible tell us about the birth of Jesus and the family of Jesus?

Jesus was born to a young virgin named Mary in the city of Bethlehem in the land of Israel. God sent an angel to Mary and told her that she, though a virgin, would give birth to a baby boy. The angel told Mary that the child would be conceived by the Holy Spirit of God without any involvement on the part of any man. After the angel came to Mary and told her about the coming birth of her child, he went to a man named Joseph who was engaged to Mary. Joseph was a humble and God-fearing carpenter in the city of Nazareth where both he and Mary lived.

The angel told Joseph that Mary had become pregnant through the work of the Holy Spirit. Joseph was shocked by the announcement and planned to break off his relationship with Mary quietly to protect both Mary and the baby. However, the angel told Joseph that he should marry Mary but that they should not live together as husband and wife until after the baby was born. Joseph and Mary accepted the message of the angel and did what he told them.

Because both Joseph and Mary were in the line of King David, they had to go the city of David called Bethlehem to enroll and pay taxes. Bethlehem was about 70 miles away from Nazareth. Joseph and pregnant Mary made the long journey together. When the young couple came to Bethlehem, they found that there were so many visitors in town that there was no place for them to stay. An innkeeper offered a stable for a resting place for them and it was here in this very humble place that Jesus was born. Mary and Joseph later had to flee to the land of Egypt with their baby boy to escape the wrath of King Herod who tried to kill Jesus. Herod was very jealous of Jesus and saw him as a potential threat to his throne. After King Herod died, Mary and Joseph and Jesus returned to Israel and went to the city of Nazareth where Jesus lived until he was about 30 years old. See Matthew 1 and 2 and Luke 1-3 for additional information about the birth, family, and ancestry of Jesus.

Sometime after Jesus was born, Mary gave birth to a number of sons and daughters with whom Jesus grew up. (See Matthew 13:55-56). Roman Catholics, however, believe that Mary stayed a virgin for her entire life, so they teach that the persons referred to as Jesus' "brothers" and "sisters" were really his cousins or possibly children of Joseph by an earlier marriage. But the Bible does not teach this.

The birth of Jesus was clearly foretold in various passages of the Old Testament. Isaiah 7:14 foretells that the coming Messiah would be born to a virgin. Micah 5:2 foretells that the Messiah (or Christ) would be born in Bethlehem. Both Matthew and Luke tell us that Jesus was born in the family line of King David. Matthew 1 focuses on the family history of Joseph who was regarded as the legal father of Jesus while Luke gives us the family history of Mary.

4. What does Philippians 2:5-7 teach us about Jesus?

This passage teaches that the person we know in history as Jesus of Nazareth actually lived in heaven as the Son of God before he came to earth. However, he voluntarily gave up his glory and many of his privileges and appeared on this earth in the form of a human baby. He came to earth as a servant so that he might redeem men from punishment and enable all those who believed in him to inherit eternal life.

When Jesus was on earth, therefore, he was truly a human person just like all other humans except for the important fact that he was completely without sin of any kind. At the same time, he was also the eternal Son of God who frequently exhibited divine knowledge, wisdom, and power. Sometimes his life clearly demonstrated his humanity. For example, he became tired, hungry, and thirsty, and experienced suffering, pain, rejection, sorrow, and misunderstanding. At other times he demonstrated that he was also divine as he healed the sick, raised the dead, multiplied food for the multitudes, knew what people were thinking, foretold the future, and forgave sinners.

In the Gospel accounts, therefore, we find passages which clearly show that Jesus did "empty" himself of some of his divine prerogatives—as taught Philippians 2:5-7. In reading other stories in the Gospels, however, we recognize that Jesus, though human, was also divine. We should never forget either Jesus' humanity or his divinity.

5. What does Philippians 2:10-11 teach us about Jesus?

Someday Jesus will be glorified by all people who have ever lived. They will bow down before him and recognize and acknowledge who he is and what he did. Everyone will *confess that Jesus Christ is Lord to the glory of God the Father*. This will be a fantastic time when all those who ignored Jesus or opposed him or doubted him or denied him or defamed him will openly and publicly acknowledge that Jesus is truly the Lord of lords and the King of kings. This does not mean that everyone will be saved. Many will not be. However, Jesus will finally receive the recognition and honor due him as the Son of God and the Son of Man—true God and true man—who is worthy of glory and honor and praise forever.

6. What does Isaiah 7:14 teach about the coming Savior?

Isaiah lived about 700 years before the birth of Christ. He foretold that the Savior to come would be born of a virgin and would be called Immanuel, which means God with us. Though many people living in Isaiah's time may not have understood the full significance of Isaiah's prediction, Matthew 1:22-23 clearly states that Jesus' birth fulfilled Isaiah's prophecy. Since Matthew wrote first of all to the Jewish people, he emphasized how the birth of Jesus fulfilled the prophecy of one of their best known prophets (Isaiah). Luke also indicates that Mary was a virgin when she became pregnant with her child (Luke 1:26-35). In Luke's account we have the clear statement that he would be called *the Son of the Most High*.

7. **When Jesus was on earth, he did many mighty and wonderful miracles. Why did so many people oppose him and reject him when he did so many good things?**

The ones who were strongest in opposing Jesus were usually people with some kind of religious authority. A group called Sadducees opposed Jesus since Jesus accepted the entire Old Testament as the Word of God and they didn't. They may also have seen Jesus as someone who was upsetting the Roman authorities with whom they (the wealthy Sadducees) often had a good relationship. The Pharisees often opposed Jesus because many of them were self-righteous and felt that they did not need Jesus for anything. (See, for example, Luke 18:11-12.) They also saw Jesus as someone who frequently broke God's law (as they understood it) and, in their minds, was therefore leading the people astray. (See, for example, Matthew 9:11, 12:2; Matthew 12:24; Matthew 15:1-2; and many others.)

The Pharisees also were alarmed and jealous that Jesus was becoming increasingly popular (John 4:1; John 7:32). They felt that Jesus was standing in the way of their own personal goals for power and authority. They were also disturbed because of the things Jesus taught about money, since the Pharisees *were lovers of money* (Luke 16:14.) Jesus therefore strongly warned the people against the teachings of the Pharisees and the Sadducees (Matthew 16:6, 11, 12). Because of their hypocrisy and self-righteousness, Jesus frequently spoke against them, thus arousing them to even greater anger and hatred. (See, for example, Jesus' exceedingly strong statements in Matthew 23:1-36.)

Some of the common people also disbelieved in Jesus (John 5:38, 6:36, 10:26, 12:37), partly because of the influence of the religious leaders. However, many others eagerly followed Jesus and believed in him. They listened to what he taught, rejoiced in his miracles, and followed him from one place to another. (See, for example, Matthew 4:25, 7:25, 8:1, 13:2, 19:2, 21:9; Mark 2:12, 6:2; 10:l; Luke 5:15, 8:42, 11:29, 14:25; John 2:22-23, 4:39, 4:53, 7:31,32, 10:42, 12:42, 16:27). The people did not always follow Jesus for the right reasons, but many of them were deeply impressed with what he said and did, and they followed him wherever he went.

Eventually, it was the Jewish religious leaders who convinced the Roman authorities that Jesus should be put to death. (See John 7:32; Matthew 26:57, 59.)

8. Why do many people reject or oppose Jesus today?

There are many different reasons why so many people oppose or reject Jesus. Some people know very little about him, and what they claim to know is often not true. Other people think that Jesus' claims for himself (the Son of God, the Savior of the world, the only way to God) are far too strong. Others believe that the teachings of Jesus are not as good and as helpful as the things they have been taught all their lives by their parents and teachers. Some believe that the Bible is not trustworthy or true. Still others do not like (or agree with) Jesus' teachings about sin and everyone's need to repent and confess their sins to a holy and righteous God.

Many others teach that Jesus was far too strict and are very displeased with his condemnation of many of the vices they enjoy. Jesus also stressed that no one can come to the Father except through himself, and that seems to them to be very arrogant and self-centered and far too restrictive. Many people feel absolutely no need for a Savior, since they consider their own lives to be "good enough" to earn for themselves a place in heaven.

Many people have never read most of the Bible and look upon it as something of an "antique" which has little relevance for people who live in the 21st century. They do not like the Bible's teaching about creation or its emphasis on man's selfishness and basic sinfulness. So, since they don't have a sense of need, they do not look for or long for a way out of their need. If there really is a God, they are quite sure that they don't have any reason to fear him or his judgment. They are quite confident they can do all that might be necessary without the help of anyone else. These are some common reasons why so many people today do not believe in Jesus as the only way to salvation or why they do not believe that they even need salvation.

9. Why did a perfect Savior have to die, even though he was totally sinless?

Jesus did not die because of anything he had done or failed to do. He lived a perfect life with absolutely no sin or failure of any kind. Precisely because he was sinless himself, he did not have to atone for any of his own sins AND he was able to die in our place as a perfect substitute for us. Hebrews 4:15 reads: *We do not have a high priest who is unable to sympathize with our weaknesses, but one who in every respect has been tempted as we are, yet without sin.* 2 Corinthians 5:21 teaches*: For our sake he made him [Jesus]to be sin who knew no sin, so that in him [Jesus] we might become the righteousness of God.* And in Hebrews 2:14-17 we read: *Since therefore the children [human beings] share in flesh and blood, he himself likewise partook of the same things, that through death he might destroy the one who has the power of death, that is, the devil, and deliver all those who through fear of death were subject to lifelong slavery. . . . He had to be made like his brothers in every respect, so that he might become a merciful and faithful high priest in the service of God, to make propitiation for the sins of the people.*

10. If you had only 20 minutes to talk to someone about Jesus, what are some of the things you would tell them?

Different Christians might emphasize different things. Some of them will emphasize those truths about Jesus which were particularly significant in their own conversion. Others might emphasize some important truths which they feel are sometimes neglected. Still others might emphasize truths about Jesus which are often misunderstood or misrepresented. The answer to this question depends somewhat on who you are and on whom you are telling about Jesus.

In general, however, it is important to include most of the following teachings—as time and circumstances permit. Jesus is the eternal and uncreated Son of God. He came to earth as a Jewish baby born to a Jewish virgin named Mary, who became pregnant through a special act of the Holy Spirit. Jesus had no earthly father, but he was brought up in the home of a carpenter named Joseph, who married Mary after she became pregnant. Jesus lived for about 33 years in the land of Israel, where he taught large numbers of people, performed many wonderful miracles, lived a perfect, sinless life, and eventually died on a cross at the hands of Roman soldiers. Though Jesus was declared to be perfectly innocent by a Roman official, the jealous religious leaders of the Jewish people persuaded the Roman governor to hand Jesus over to the soldiers to be crucified. After three days, Jesus rose again from the dead, remained on earth for 40 more days, demonstrating that he had conquered death and teaching about God's kingship. Then he returned in glory to his Father in heaven where he reigns over the entire world. Because Jesus was perfectly sinless, he willingly and voluntarily died on the cross as a substitute to pay the penalty for the sins of all those who put their faith and trust in him. Someday Jesus will come back to earth again to judge all people and to reign forever in glory with all those who loved and trusted and served him.

Lesson Five: Salvation

Introduction

In Lesson Four we learned about the wonderful things that Jesus Christ said and did while he was on earth. However, you may wonder what all this has to do with *you*. You may be asking: "Did Jesus die in *my* place? Can I find forgiveness for all *my* sins? Can I really be sure that *I* will live forever with Jesus in glory?" In this Lesson you will read the Bible's answer to those questions.

1. What does it mean to be "saved"?

Being saved is not the same as being baptized or joining a church or making a public profession of faith. Being saved involves an inward change in a person's mind and heart which is brought about by the work of the Holy Spirit in his life. A person who is saved sincerely trusts in Jesus Christ as the one who paid the penalty for his sins and accepts Jesus as the Lord and Master of his life. A saved person is therefore a child of God whose sins have all been forgiven and who has received the gift of eternal life.

Scripture References

To all who did receive him [Jesus], who believed in his name, he gave the right to become children of God. (John 1:12)
The blood of Jesus his Son cleanses us from all sin. (1 John 1:7)
God gave us eternal life, and this life is in his Son. (1 John 5:11)

2. How can God forgive us without punishing us?

God forgives us because Jesus Christ, the sinless Son of God, took on himself the punishment which we deserved. When we put our trust in Jesus and accept him as our Savior, he becomes our substitute. God accepts Jesus' sacrifice on the cross in our behalf and declares *us* not guilty.

Scripture References

He was pierced for our transgressions, he was crushed for our iniquities; upon him was the chastisement that brought us peace, and with his wounds we are healed. (Isaiah 53:5)

For God so loved the world that he gave his only Son, that whoever believes in him should not perish but have eternal life. (John 3:16)

He himself bore our sins in his body on the tree, that we might die to sin and live to righteousness. By his wounds you have been healed. (1 Peter 2:24)

All have sinned and fall short of the glory of God, and are justified by his grace as a gift, through the redemption that is in Christ Jesus, whom God put forward as a propitiation by his blood, to be received by faith. (Romans 3:23-25)

3. Is God actually willing to forgive all our sins?

Yes, every one! There is no sin too great or too serious to be beyond God's forgiving grace. However, we should remember that God's gracious forgiveness does not always repair the harm that is done in this life because of our sins. The *guilt* of our sin is gone, but the *consequences* of our sin may continue in many different ways.

Scripture References

Though your sins are like scarlet, they shall be as white as snow; though they are red like crimson, they shall become like wool. (Isaiah 1:18)

As far as the east is from the west, so far does he remove our transgressions from us. (Psalm 103:12)

He [God] will again have compassion on us; he will tread our iniquities underfoot. You will cast all our sins into the depths of the sea. (Micah 7:19)

4. What must I do in order to receive this wonderful salvation?

You must humbly repent of your sins and sincerely believe that Jesus died in *your* place. Faith is not simply a mental belief that Jesus died on the cross for "the sins of the world." It is a sincere belief that Jesus died specifically for *you*. It also includes treasuring Jesus as supremely precious, desiring to have Jesus take control of your life, and sincerely committing yourself to please and honor him in all that you do.

Scripture References
The apostle Paul said: *Testifying both to Jews and to Greeks of repentance toward God and of faith in our Lord Jesus Christ. (Acts 20:21)*
Repent therefore, and turn again, that your sins may be blotted out. (Acts 3:19)
Believe in the Lord Jesus, and you will be saved, you and your household. (Acts 16:31)

5. What does it mean to repent?

To repent involves honestly admitting that we have not lived the way God wants us to live, sincerely grieving over the ways we dishonor God and hurt others through our failures and sins, truly desiring to stay away from those sins in the future, and genuinely intending to live the rest of our lives the way God wants us to live. We may have to repent over and over again, but our sincere desire and intention is to increasingly do the will of God through the help of the Holy Spirit.

Scripture References
Have mercy on me, O God, according to your steadfast love; according to your abundant mercy blot out my transgressions . . . wash me, and I shall be whiter than snow . . . Hide your face from my sins and blot out all my iniquities. Create in me a clean heart, O God, and renew a right spirit within me . . . Restore to me the joy of your salvation, and uphold me with a willing spirit. (Psalm 51:1,7, 9-10, 12)
The apostle Paul said, *"I declared that they should repent and turn to God, performing deeds in keeping with their repentance." (Acts 26:20)*

6. Can't we earn salvation by simply doing our best to live a good life?

No. If we do not truly love Jesus and put our trust in him, even our best works will merit nothing. Salvation is a gift of God's mercy and grace. It is impossible to merit it or earn it. Besides, even if we committed only one sin (and we all commit far more), we would have to pay the penalty for that sin. And, *the wages of sin is death* (Romans 6:23).

Scripture References
There is none who does good, not even one. (Psalm 53:3)
We know that a person is not justified by works of the law but through faith in Jesus Christ, so we also have believed in Christ Jesus, in order to be justified by faith in Christ and not by works of the law, because by works of the law no one will be justified. (Galatians 2:16)
God, being rich in mercy, because of the great love with which he loved us, even when we were dead in our trespasses, made us alive together with Christ . . . For by grace you have been saved through faith. And this is not your own doing; it is the gift of God, not a result of works, so that no one may boast. (Ephesians 2:4-5, 8-9)

7. Is there another way to be saved if we do not believe in Jesus?

No. Many people have tried to find another way through punishing themselves, showing kindness to others, giving gifts to the poor, making some significant personal sacrifices, serving other gods, or simply doing the best they can. But none of these things will erase our sins or give us peace with God.

Scripture References
Jesus said, *"I am the way, and the truth, and the life. No one comes to the Father except through me." (John 14:6)*
All the prophets bear witness that everyone who believes in him [Jesus] receives forgiveness of sins through his name. (Acts 10:43)
For there is one God, and there is one mediator between God and

men, the man Christ Jesus, who gave himself as a ransom for all. (1 Timothy 2:5-6)

There is salvation in no one else, for there is no other name under heaven given among men by which we must be saved. (Acts 4:12)

Whoever does not believe God has made him a liar, because he has not believed in the testimony that God has borne concerning his Son. And this is the testimony, that God gave us eternal life, and this life is in his Son. Whoever has the Son has life; whoever does not have the Son of God does not have life. (1 John 5:10-12)

8. What does the Bible teach about being born again?

No one can be saved unless he is born again. This involves a radical change in our lives which no one can accomplish by himself any more than a person can arrange for his own natural birth.

Scripture Reference

Jesus said, *"Truly, truly, I say to you, unless one is born again he cannot see the kingdom of God." (John 3:3)*

You have been born again, not of perishable seed but of imperishable, through the living and abiding word of God. (1 Peter 1:23)

9. What does it mean to be born again?

To be born again is to receive a new, inner spiritual life through the Holy Spirit. When that happens, the believer becomes a new creation in Christ and a child of God. (See Lesson Six for more information about the Holy Spirit.)

Scripture References

Jesus said, *"That which is born of the flesh is flesh, and that which is born of the Spirit is spirit. Do not marvel that I said to you, 'You must be born again.'" (John 3:6-7)*

To all who did receive him [Jesus], who believed in his name, he gave the right to become children of God, who were born, not of

blood nor of the will of the flesh nor of the will of man, but of God. (John 1:12-13)
No one born of God makes a practice of sinning, for God's seed abides in him, and he cannot keep on sinning because he has been born of God. (1 John 3:9)
Everyone who believes that Jesus is the Christ has been born of God. (1 John 5:1)
If anyone is in Christ, he is a new creation. The old has passed away; behold, the new has come! (2 Corinthians 5:17)

10. Why is it necessary for someone to be born again in order to enter the kingdom of heaven?

Without the new birth, we are all spiritually dead, born under the sentence of death, and deserving of God's punishment. Unless we are spiritually changed in our hearts and minds through the work of the Holy Spirit, we remain under the sentence of death.

Scripture References
Behold, I was brought forth in iniquity, and in sin did my mother conceive me. (Psalm 51:5)
You were dead in the trespasses and sins in which you once walked, following the course of this world . . . We all once lived in the passions of our flesh, carrying out the desires of the body and the mind, and were by nature children of wrath, like the rest of mankind. (Ephesians 2:1-3)
And you, who were dead in your trespasses . . . God made alive together with him (Christ). (Colossians 2:13)

11. What great blessings are given to everyone who is born again?

Everyone who sincerely repents of his sins and trusts in Jesus as Savior becomes a child of God. He receives the gift of eternal life and is no longer under the sentence of death because of his sins. He also is given a genuine desire to live for God in a way that pleases and honors him.

Scripture References

Jesus said, *"Truly, truly, I say to you, whoever hears my word and believes him who sent me has eternal life. He does not come into judgment, but has passed from death to life." (John 5:24)*

If you confess with your mouth that Jesus is Lord and believe in your heart that God raised him from the dead, you will be saved. (Romans 10:9)

To all who did receive him, who believed in his name, he gave the right to become children of God. (John 1:12)

These are written so that you may believe that Jesus is the Christ, the Son of God, and that by believing you may have life in his name. (John 20:31)

12. What is eternal life and when does it begin?

Eternal life is not simply a life that does not end. Eternal life involves a new relationship between a believer and God. It is a relationship of love, joy, and peace that begins the moment someone believes in Jesus and will never end. Through faith the eternal life of God enters into us as the Holy Spirit of God comes into our hearts.

Scripture References

Jesus said, *"Truly, truly, I say to you, whoever believes has eternal life." (John 6:47)*

This is eternal life, that they know you the only true God, and Jesus Christ, whom you have sent. (John 17:3)

It is no longer I who live, but Christ who lives in me. (Galatians 2:20)

By this we know that he abides in us, by the Spirit whom he has given us. (1 John 3:24)

13. If we believe in Christ, is it important for us to confess our faith publicly and also to be baptized?

Yes. Public confession of our faith in Jesus and water baptism are both very important. However, there may be times when a person chooses not to make a public profession of faith or be baptized immediately. This might be true, for example, when a

82

public profession of faith would alienate family or friends whom the new convert is trying to reach with the Gospel. Or a public baptism might result in significant persecution which would remove a mother or father or young person from their home. It is important that we do not deny Christ, but we may have to be prudent in choosing a time and place for our baptism.

Scripture References
Jesus said, *"Everyone who acknowledges me before men, I also will acknowledge before my Father who is in heaven, but whoever denies me before men, I also will deny before my Father who is in heaven." (Matthew 10:32-33)*
Repent and be baptized every one of you in the name of Jesus Christ for the forgiveness of your sins. (Acts 2:38)
When they believed Philip as he preached good news about the kingdom of God and the name of Jesus Christ, they were baptized, both men and women. (Acts 8:12)
If you confess with your mouth that Jesus is Lord and believe in your heart that God raised him from the dead, you will be saved. For with the heart one believes and is justified, and with the mouth one confesses and is saved. (Romans 10:9-10)

14. Can we be absolutely sure that we are saved for eternity?

Yes. God's promises are sure, so we never have to doubt them. Even when we fail at times to live the way God wants us to live (or fail to live as we ourselves want to live), we may be sure that God will continue to love us and forgive us when we truly put our trust in Jesus.

Scripture References
Jesus said: *"I give them eternal life, and they will never perish, and no one will snatch them out of my hand." (John 10:28)*
I write these things to you who believe in the name of the Son of God that you may know that you have eternal life. (1 John 5:13)
If we confess our sins, he is faithful and just to forgive us our sins and to cleanse us from all unrighteousness. (1 John 1:9)
For I am sure that neither death nor life, nor angels nor rulers, nor things present nor things to come, nor powers, nor height nor

depth, nor anything else in all creation, will be able to separate us from the love of God in Christ Jesus our Lord. (Romans 8:38-39)

Exploring Further

1. What does it mean to be saved?

In general, we refer to salvation as something that takes place only once in a person's life. One cannot be saved today and lost tomorrow and then be saved over and over again. Salvation is not the same as forgiveness. A person can be forgiven over and over again (and all believers are forgiven repeatedly), but truly saved only once. Salvation involves the sincere confession of our sins and a sincere profession of faith in Jesus Christ as the one who died on the cross to pay the penalty for our sins. When we sincerely confess and profess these things, we become children of God, our sins are forgiven, and we are given the gift of eternal life. We may still sin at times after we are saved and we may also lose our sense of the blessedness and joy of our salvation, but sin by itself does not take away our position as saved children of our heavenly Father. By sincerely confessing our sins and humbly asking for forgiveness, we can again be restored to a right relationship to God. We obviously should never take our sins lightly or act as if they don't matter very much. However, we should not let our sins and weaknesses destroy our confidence that we truly belong to Christ in spite of those weaknesses. Recall the words of David in Psalm 51 after he was guilty of the sins of adultery and murder: *Wash me, and I shall be whiter than snow. Let me hear joy and gladness . . . Hide your face from my sins, and blot out all my iniquities. Create in me a clean heart, O God, and renew a right spirit within me . . . Restore to me the joy of your salvation, and uphold me with a willing spirit. (Psalm 51:7-12)*

2. What must a person do to be saved?

We must sincerely confess our sins, demonstrate true repentance for what we have done or failed to do, and put our complete trust in Jesus and his sacrifice to atone for all our sins. It is very important, however, to realize that salvation is a gift and is not something we earn or merit. By confessing our sins and putting our trust in Jesus, we acknowledge that there is nothing we can do by ourselves to atone for our sins or make ourselves right with God. We do not simply promise that we will change our conduct and start walking on a new path and then assume that God will be satisfied with our good intentions or sincere promises. Rather, when we humbly confess our sins and place our trust in Jesus, we throw ourselves on his mercy with the acknowledgement that there is absolutely nothing we can do to win the favor of God or earn the gift of salvation.

Salvation is therefore always and completely a work of God's GRACE rather than the result of human effort. It may be significant when a person sincerely says, "I'll do better from now on," but that is much different from recognizing our own inability to get right with God through our own efforts. The apostle Paul carefully obeyed all God's Old Testament laws when he was younger, describing himself in Philippians 3:6 as someone who was "faultless" in regard to legal righteousness. However, in regard to salvation Paul wrote, *But God, being rich in mercy, because of the great love with which he loved us, even when we were dead in our trespasses, made us alive together with Christ—by grace you have been saved. (Ephesians 2:4-5)* A bit later he added: *For by grace you have been saved through faith. And this is not your own doing; it is the gift of God, not a result of works, so that no one may boast. For we are his workmanship, created in Christ Jesus for good works, which God prepared beforehand, that we should walk in them. (Ephesians 2:8-9)*

3. Can a person be saved without knowing it? Can a person think he is saved without really being saved?

The answer to both questions is YES. A person who is saved definitely should know that he is saved, without doubt or hesitation. However, there are people who are genuinely sorry for their sins and who sincerely trust in Jesus for salvation who still sometimes doubt that they are truly saved. This is particularly true when people focus on their own weaknesses and failures rather than focusing on the perfect life and atoning sacrifice of Jesus. They may feel that they simply are not good enough to be a child of God and they deeply regret that they still wrestle with significant sins in their lives. All believers should regret any sin in their lives, but they should not focus so much on their sins that they forget the many promises in the Bible that God will truly forgive all those who sincerely repent of their sins and trust him to forgive them all. As Isaiah 1:18 teaches: *Though your sins are like scarlet, they shall be as white as snow; though they are red like crimson, they shall become like wool.* And 1 John 1:9 teaches: *If we confess our sins, he is faithful and just to forgive us our sins and to cleanse us from all unrighteousness.*

It is also possible for people to believe they are saved when they are not. Regrettably, there are many people like that. These people often take sin very lightly and therefore believe that they have nothing to worry about. They often overestimate their own holiness and underestimate their own sinfulness. They do not put their trust in Jesus alone, since they feel they don't need a Savior. They often have a sense of self-righteousness and believe that they are much better than most other people. And even if they do recognize that they are not as good as they should be, many feel that God is a very kind and gracious being who really doesn't take sin very seriously. In his sight (they argue), no one is so bad that he should suffer any significant punishment for whatever sins he might happen to have done.

These people are in a far worse situation than those who truly believe in Jesus but aren't living the kind of holy life they would like to live. Those who are not absolutely sure of their salvation often tend to underestimate the mercy and kindness and grace of God, while those who don't feel a need for a Savior tend to overestimate their own goodness while underestimating God's holiness and righteousness. At one time the apostle Paul had much confidence in his own righteousness. However, when he came to know Jesus and put his faith in him, he realized that in God's sight he had not been righteous at all (Philippians 3:4-9).

4. What is meant by "substitutionary atonement"?

This phrase refers to the teaching that Jesus died on the cross to pay the penalty for our sins. That is, Jesus was our substitute when he died on the cross. We could never pay the penalty for our sins, so we needed a perfect Savior who was willing to die in our place so that our sins might be forgiven and God could look on us with favor instead of wrath. Romans 3:25 states this truth in these words: *God put forward [Jesus] as a propitiation by his blood.*

1 John 4:10 focuses on the love of God in substitutionary atonement: *This is love, not that we have loved God but that he loved us and sent his Son to be the propitiation for our sins.* "Propitation" means a sacrifice that God lovingly provides, a sacrifice that endures God's wrath against sin and brings the sinner into God's favor and acceptance. Romans 5:10 states: *While we were [God's] enemies we were reconciled to God by the death of his Son.* We deserved to die because of our sin, but we could never pay the penalty for our sins and still live. Jesus therefore became our substitute, our sacrifice of propitiation. Since he had no sins to pay for, he and he alone could pay the penalty we deserve and still live!

After Jesus died and was buried, he arose again on the third day and returned to his Father in heaven. When the devil, the great accuser, wants to call attention to our sins, Jesus is there in the presence of the Father to declare that all our sins have already been paid for. As Romans 6:23 teaches, *The wages of sin is death, but the free gift of God is eternal life in Christ Jesus our Lord.* We can therefore live all the days of our life on earth in gratitude, joy, and obedience for what Jesus has done for us as our perfect substitute.

The phrase *substitutionary atonement* is not found in most Bible translations. However, the idea of substitutionary atonement is found in every translation. It is at the very heart of the gospel. Included among the relevant Scripture passages are the following:

He [Jesus] was pierced for our transgressions; he was crushed for our iniquities; upon him was the chastisement that brought us peace, and with his wounds we are healed. All we like sheep have gone astray; we have turned—every one -- to his own way; and the Lord has laid on him the iniquity of us all. (Isaiah 53:5-6)

Christ redeemed us from the curse of the law by becoming a curse for us. (Galatians 3:13)

He [Jesus] committed no sin . . . He himself bore our sins in his body on the tree [cross], that we might die to sin and live to righteousness. By his wounds you have been healed. (I Peter 2:23,24)

Christ also suffered once for sins, the righteous for the unrighteous, that he might bring us to God. (1 Peter 3:18)

In this is love, not that we have loved God but that he loved us and sent his Son to be the propitiation for our sins. (1 John 4:10)

He [Jesus] is able to save to the uttermost those who draw near to God through him, since he always lives to make intercession for them. (Hebrews 7:25)

Christ Jesus is the one who died—more than that, who was raised—who is at the right hand of God, who indeed is interceding for us. (Romans 8:34)

5. If someone does not believe in Jesus, is there some other way he can be saved?

NO. Jesus is the only way to salvation. There is no other. Jesus himself said: *"I am the way, and the truth, and the life. No one comes to the Father except through me"* (John 14:6). Jesus also said, *"I am the bread of life; whoever comes to me shall not hunger, and whoever believes in me shall never thirst"* (John 6:35). On another occasion Jesus said: *"I am the door of the sheep. All who came before me are thieves and robbers . . I am the door. If anyone enters by me, he will be saved . . . I am the good shepherd. The good shepherd lays down his life for the sheep. . . . I know my own and my own know me . . . and I lay down my life for the sheep"* (John 10:7-15).

Throughout history there has never been any one else like Jesus. Only Jesus was perfect and totally free from sin (1 John 3:5; Hebrews 4:15). Only Jesus had the love and holiness and ability to give his life to pay for the sins of others. And no one else had the power to rise again from the dead. Jesus said: *"For this reason the Father loves me, because I lay down my life that I may take it up again. No one takes it from me, but I lay it down of my own accord. I have authority to lay it down, and I have authority to take it up again."* (John 10:17-18)

Very young children, of course, do not fully understand who Jesus was or what he did. But they still love and trust him and believe that he died for them. Even many older people have little knowledge or understanding of Jesus, but they do believe in him and trust him to be their Savior. Jesus himself said that we must become like little children (in humility, faith and trust) in order to enter the kingdom of heaven. (See Matthew 11:25, 18:3, 19:14.) It is Jesus who saves us—not our own efforts or knowledge. Anyone who is saved (at any time or any place) will be saved only because of what Jesus did when he lived a perfect life and died for the sins of those who put their trust in him. Jesus and Jesus alone is the perfect Savior—whether our knowledge of him is small or great.

6. What does it mean to be spiritually dead? Are all people spiritually dead unless they are born again?

A spiritually dead person is someone who is not saved. He has not been born again. Christ does not live in him. He has only the old "sin nature" with which everyone is born. Many people who are spiritually dead are self-centered, immoral, proud, foolish, and disobedient. However, spiritually dead people are not necessarily "bad" people in the sense that they are always violating the law or hurting others or robbing people or treating them disrespectfully. Some of them may actually be kind, friendly, helpful and pleasant to live with. However, they do not serve others out of love for God, they do not trust in Jesus, they do not seek to live according to the teachings of God's Word, they do not put Christ first in their lives, they do not acknowledge or confess their sins before God, and they do not seek to live to the praise and honor of God. By human standards some of them may be considered "good" and worthy of praise. However, they do not have the love or the life of Christ in their hearts and they do not seek to live to the glory of God. They are spiritually lost.

Ephesians 2:1-3 puts it this way: *You were dead in the trespasses and sins in which you once walked, following the course of this world, following the prince of the power of the air [Satan], the spirit that is now at work in the sons of disobedience—among whom we all once lived in the passions of our flesh, carrying out the desires of the body and the mind, and were by nature children of wrath, like the rest of mankind.* Likewise, Colossians 2:13 reads: *You, who were dead in your trespasses . . . God made alive together with him.* Revelation 3:1 says: *You have the reputation of being alive, but you are dead.* According to the Bible, therefore, every person who is not born again is spiritually dead.

7. **What does it mean to be born again? Can we somehow earn the privilege of being born again? Can a person be born again more than once?**

To be born again means to receive new spiritual life from the Holy Spirit. It cannot be earned or merited by anything we do. It is a gift of God. And, just as we can be born physically only once, we can be spiritually "born again" only once.

Being born again involves the miraculous, spiritual, and somewhat "mysterious" work of the Holy Spirit in a person's life. When a person is born again, it is as if the "seed" of new spiritual life is planted in the center of his life. He has a conviction of sin which drives him to genuine repentance, sincere faith in the atoning work of Jesus, a new purpose for living, a heartfelt desire to do what God wants him to do, a deep love for Jesus, and a genuine love for others. Being born again also brings a heart of joy, thanksgiving, and a new spirit of praise and gratitude in a person's life. The following passages all refer to this new birth.

> Jesus said: *Unless one is born of water and the Spirit, he cannot enter the kingdom of God. That which is born of the flesh is flesh, and that which is born of the Spirit is spirit. (John 3:5-6)*
>
> *If anyone is in Christ, he is a new creation. The old has passed away; behold, the new has come. (2 Corinthians 5:17)*
>
> *[You] were taught in him, as the truth is in Jesus, to put off your old self, which belongs to your former manner of life and is corrupt through deceitful desires, and to be renewed in the spirit of your minds, and to put on the new self, created after the likeness of God in true righteousness and holiness. (Ephesians 4:22-24)*
>
> *You have put off the old self with its practices and have put on the new self, which is being renewed in knowledge after the image of its creator. (Colossians 3:9-10)*
>
> *Blessed be the God and Father of our Lord Jesus Christ! According to his great mercy, he has caused us to be born again to a living hope . . . to an inheritance that is imperishable, undefiled, and unfading. (1 Peter 1:3-4)*

People who are born again are made new spiritually and have a sincere desire to serve God in every area of their lives. However, they are not yet perfect in this life. They still sin and fall short of being all they want to be or hope to be. As long as they are on this earth, they will still have to wrestle with failure and temptation. However, even if they do fail at times, they do not lose their status as children of God who are truly in Christ and destined for an eternity of joy and peace and love in his presence.

There are five important theological terms which describe various aspects of our salvation: regeneration, conversion, justification, sanctification, and glorification.

• **Regeneration** describes being born again.

- **Conversion** describes the initial radical change in our lives when we turn away from living a sinful life that dishonors and displeases God to a life that honors and pleases him.

- **Justification** describes our standing before the judgment seat of God as people who are *declared* by God himself to be "not guilty." God counts Jesus' goodness as ours and counts our sins as paid for by Jesus. Even though we may still need to be cleansed over and over again, we as believers in Jesus are declared "justified" or "not guilty" because Jesus paid the penalty for all of our sins—past, present, and future, and because Jesus' perfect obedience is forever counted as ours.

- **Sanctification** describes the *process* of becoming more holy in our lives through the work of the Holy Spirit who dwells within us. Sanctification is a lifelong process which is never fully completed until the day of our death or Jesus' return.

- **Glorification** describes the *future* glory which we will experience when we will be with Christ forever in glory. We will have perfect new bodies and will forever be without sin or sickness or sadness of any kind. We will also experience joy and love and peace far beyond anything we have ever experienced before.

According to the Bible, our SALVATION includes regeneration, conversion, justification, sanctification and ultimately glorification.

8. What is meant by eternal life? Does this refer simply to the length of life or does it refer to something more than that?

The phrase "eternal life" does not always refer to exactly the same thing. "Eternal life" sometimes refers to a life that never ends. In that sense, "eternal life" is the same as "everlasting life." However, "eternal life" may also refer to a new quality of life, a life in Christ that is far superior to life without Christ. This life, too, does not end, but the emphasis is more on the kind of life that a believer experiences rather than on the fact that it has no end. In some Bible translations the phrases "eternal life" and "everlasting life" seem to be used interchangeably. Consider the following passages.

> *This is eternal life, that they know you the only true God, and Jesus Christ whom you have sent. (John 17:3)*
> Jesus said: *"Whoever hears my word and believes him who sent me has eternal life. He does not come into judgment, but has passed from death to life." (John 5:24)*
> Jesus said, *"There is no one who has left house or wife or brothers or parents or children, for the sake of the kingdom of God, who will not receive many times more in this time, and in the age to come eternal life." (Luke 18:29-30)*
> Jesus said, *"These [the unrighteous] will go away into eternal punishment, but the righteous into eternal life." (Matthew 25:46)*
> *Everyone who hates his brother is a murderer, and you know that no murderer has eternal life abiding in him. (1 John 3:15)*
> *For God so loved the world, that he gave his only Son, that whoever believes in him should not perish but have eternal life. (John 3:16)*

9. Can a person be saved without being baptized? Can a person be baptized without being saved? Why is baptism important?

The answer to the first two questions is YES. Some people are truly saved but for one reason or another choose not be baptized (at least, not for a while). Perhaps they put off baptism because they are afraid of the reactions of family or friends or government authorities if they are baptized. Some may consider that baptism is not really important or required since they emphasize the "baptism of the Holy Spirit." Still others may live in a place or situation where there is no one to baptize them.

Many others are baptized out of tradition or the expectations of family or friends but do not have a true saving relationship with Jesus Christ. Many children are also baptized but never come to the point where they commit their lives to Jesus.

Why is baptism important? First, because Jesus commanded believers to be baptized (Matthew 28:19). In the early church there appeared to be no questions about the importance of Christian baptism. Second, baptism is a sign and a seal that a person belongs to Jesus Christ, that his sins are washed away, and that he belongs to Christ in every area of his life. It is a great blessing for a person to live in this life knowing that he has received the God-appointed sign that his sins are truly washed away and that he belongs for time and eternity to his Savior Jesus Christ.

[Note: There are many churches that practice the baptism of infants as well as the baptism of professing believers (of various ages). Those who practice infant baptism do so for different reasons. Some wrongly believe that children are saved through baptism itself. Others baptize infants only if they are children of believing parents. They emphasize that children of believers in the Old Testament received the sign of circumcision according to the explicit command of God. This sign indicated that the children of believers belonged to God and thus received a sign which indicated the removal of sin and impurity. In their understanding, children of believers today should receive baptism as the New Testament sign of this spiritual blessing. It is also interesting to note that three of the relatively few stories of baptism in the New Testament involved the baptism of entire families: Acts 16:15, Acts 16:31-33, 1 Corinthians 1:16.]

Jesus said: *"Go therefore and make disciples of all nations, baptizing them in the name of the Father and of the Son and of the Holy Spirit." (Matthew 28:19)*
Peter said: *"Repent and be baptized every one of you in the name of Jesus Christ for the forgiveness of your sins. For the promise is for you and for your children and for all who are*

far off, everyone whom the Lord our God calls to himself."
(Acts 2:38-39)
As many of you as were baptized into Christ have put on
Christ. (Galatians 3:27)
In him also you were circumcised . . . by the circumcision of
Christ, having been buried with him in baptism, in which you
were also raised with him through faith in the powerful
working of God, who raised him from the dead. (Colossians
2:11-12)

See also the many examples of baptism in the early church: Acts 2:41; Acts 8:12,13,16, 38; Acts 9:18; Acts 10:48; Acts 16:15, 33; Acts 18:8; Acts 19:5; Acts 22:16. Also note in 1 Corinthians 1:13-17 where the apostle Paul indicated that he baptized very few believers, since he did not want people to focus on himself rather than on Jesus Christ. Paul was certainly not opposed to baptism itself, but he wanted new believers to recognize that Jesus is the Savior who died for them and that apostles and evangelists and preachers were just servants who proclaimed the message of salvation.

10. Is it possible to be absolutely sure of our salvation? If not, why not? If so, how do we gain this assurance?

Yes! It is possible to be sure of our salvation. Some may question this, since they know of people who at one time seemed to be saved but later left the faith and went back to another religion or to no religion at all. Others recognize that they themselves may not always be very confident of their salvation since their faith is weak at times and their lives do not always demonstrate that Christ lives within them. However, our assurance of salvation does not rest on anything that we have done or can do, but it rests completely on what CHRIST has done for us and our sincere belief in what the Bible teaches about him. If we truly believe the promises of God and humbly and sincerely confess Jesus as our Lord and Savior, then we may be sure that we are truly God's children. It's also important, however, that our lives do reflect what we claim to believe! Not only should we seek to stay away from all known sin, but we should also firmly choose to pursue only that which is pleasing to our Lord.

> *These are written that you may believe that Jesus is the Christ, the Son of God, and that by believing you may have life in his name. (John 20:31)*
> *The Spirit himself bears witness with our spirit that we are children of God. (Romans 8:16)*
> *I write these things to you who believe in the name of the Son of God that you may know that you have eternal life. . . . We know that we are from God . . . and we know that the Son of God has come and has given us understanding, so that we may know him who is true; and we are in him who is true, in his Son Jesus Christ. (1 John 5:19-20)*

11. Is it possible to feel sure of our salvation even though we are not truly saved?

Yes! There probably are many people like that. They may put their trust in the fact that they were once baptized, are members of a local church, attend the church regularly, and read the Bible and pray fairly often. However, all these activities can hide the fact that they have never truly been born again, they do not truly love the Lord with their whole heart, and they are not putting their trust for salvation in Christ alone. It is therefore important for us to examine our own hearts and lives to make sure that our confidence is never based on our own activities but rather on the finished work of Jesus on the cross and his special work in our own hearts and lives.

If our faith is weak at times and we are not living as we should, we should earnestly pray to the Lord for spiritual renewal, greater love for him, and a sincere desire to serve him in all that we do. We should also again read and study those passages in the Bible which teach us about all that Jesus has done for us so that we build our lives on the solid foundation of the truth of God as found in his holy Word.

Lesson Six: The Holy Spirit

Introduction

Before Jesus left his disciples, he promised that he would send the Holy Spirit to them when he returned to heaven. The Holy Spirit would come to them, live within them, and help them live the kind of life Jesus wanted them to live. He would also serve as their counselor and guide, bringing to their minds everything Jesus had taught them while he was on earth.

Through the Holy Spirit, the disciples and all other believers would be able to produce spiritual fruit that would glorify God. The Spirit would purify their motives, fill them with joy and help them to be all that Christ taught them to be. The Holy Spirit would also enable them to witness to others with such power that many people would be attracted to Christ and to the fellowship of believers.

1. Who is the Holy Spirit?

The Holy Spirit is God, just as the Father is God and the Son is God. Both the Old Testament and the New Testament make frequent references to the Holy Spirit. In the Old Testament he is usually referred to simply as the Spirit of God while in the New Testament he is often referred to as "the Holy Spirit." Christians refer to the Holy Spirit as the "third person" of the Holy Trinity: Father, Son and Holy Spirit.

Scripture References
"The Spirit searches everything, even the depths of God.. .. no one comprehends the thoughts of God except the Spirit of God."
1 Corinthians 2:10-11
"Do you not know that you are God's temple and that God's Spirit dwells in you?" 1 Corinthians 3:16
"God has sent the Spirit of his Son into our hearts." Galatians 4:6

2. Does this mean that there are three separate Gods called the Father and the Son and the Holy Spirit?

No. The Bible repeatedly emphasizes that there is only one true God. However, the Bible also teaches that the Father is God, the Son is God, and the Holy Spirit is God. Believers therefore refer to the one true God as the Holy Trinity (Tri-Unity or three-in-one). Though we cannot fully understand this teaching, we accept it as a truth which God has made known to us in the Bible. When we honor and worship the Father and the Son and the Holy Spirit, we are worshiping the one true God.

Scripture References
Jesus said: *"'Go therefore and make disciples of all nations, baptizing them in the name of the Father and of the Son and of the Holy Spirit.'" Matthew 28:19*

Paul wrote: *"The grace of the Lord Jesus Christ and the love of God and the fellowship of the Holy Spirit be with you all." 2 Corinthians 13:14*

3. Is the Holy Spirit a divine Person or simply a spiritual influence?

The Holy Spirit is a divine Person as the Father and the Son are. The Holy Spirit thinks, loves, feels and acts. He also comforts us, prays for us, hears our prayers, teaches and guides us, purifies us and lives within us.

Scripture References
Jesus said, *"'The Helper, the Holy Spirit, whom the Father will send in my name, he will teach you all things and bring to your remembrance all that I have said to you." John 14:26*
"The Scripture had to be fulfilled, which the Holy Spirit spoke beforehand." Acts 1:16
"'When the Spirit of truth comes, he will guide you into all the truth.'" John 16:13
"They were all filled with the Holy Spirit and began to speak in other tongues as the Spirit gave them utterance." Acts 2:4

"And do not grieve the Holy Spirit of God, by whom you were sealed for the day of redemption." Ephesians 4:30

4. When do we first read about the Holy Spirit in the Bible?

We first read about the Holy Spirit in the second verse of the Bible. The Holy Spirit was involved in the creation of the world and continues to be involved in the creation of all new life in the world.

Scripture References

"The earth was without form and void, and darkness was over the face of the deep. And the Spirit of God was hovering over the face of the waters." Genesis 1:2

"When you send forth your Spirit, they are created, and you renew the face of the ground." Psalm 104:30

5. What is the role of the Holy Spirit in our spiritual life?

The Holy Spirit is the creator and source of *spiritual* life just as he is the source of *natural* life. He produces spiritual fruit in us, leads us into the truth, gives us victory over temptation, comforts us in times of sadness and sorrow, encourages us in times of weakness, assures us of forgiveness when we sincerely confess our sins, empowers us to be faithful witnesses to Jesus, and helps us to become more like our Savior Jesus.

Scripture References

Jesus said, *"'Unless one is born of water and the Spirit, he cannot enter the kingdom of God. That which is born of the flesh is flesh, and that which is born of the Spirit is spirit.'" John 3:5-6*

"He saved us, not because of works done by us in righteousness, but according to his own mercy, by the washing of regeneration and renewal of the Holy Spirit." Titus 3:5

Jesus said, *"'You will receive power when the Holy Spirit has come upon you, and you will be my witnesses.'" Acts 1:8*

"They were all filled with the Holy Spirit and continued to speak the word of God with boldness." Acts 4:31

"Anyone who does not have the Spirit of Christ does not belong

to him." Romans 8:9

6. How can we receive the Holy Spirit into our own hearts and lives?

We must repent of our sins, trust in Jesus for forgiveness, and ask our Father in heaven to give us the gift of the Holy Spirit.

Scripture References
"'Repent and be baptized every one of you in the name of Jesus Christ for the forgiveness of your sins, and you will receive the gift of the Holy Spirit.'" Acts 2:38
"'If you then, who are evil, know how to give good gifts to your children, how much more will the heavenly Father give the Holy Spirit to those who ask him!'" Luke 11:13

7. What kind of spiritual fruit does the Holy Spirit produce in the lives of believers?

The Holy Spirit enables us to produce spiritual fruit that glorifies God and blesses others. Without the work of the Holy Spirit in our hearts and lives, we would never be able to become the kind of people God wants us to be.

Scripture References
"The fruit of the Spirit is love, joy, peace, patience, kindness, goodness, faithfulness, gentleness, self-control." Galatians 5:22-23
"Those who live according to the Spirit set their minds on the things of the Spirit.. .. to set the mind on the Spirit is life and peace." Romans 8:5- 6
"If we live by the Spirit, let us also walk by the Spirit." Galatians 5:25

8. How does the Holy Spirit help us resist and overcome temptation?

When we humbly follow the leading of the Holy Spirit, we are able to be victorious over temptations of every kind. The

Holy Spirit actually lives within us, helping us to focus on things that are pleasing to God and enabling us to resist the temptations of our flesh. The Holy Spirit may also bring to our minds truths that we have forgotten. He helps us to remember that we belong to God and that we are not our own masters. And he creates a renewed desire in our hearts to live for the Savior who died for us.

Scripture References
"Walk by the Spirit, and you will not gratify the desires of the flesh." Galatians 5:16
"You. .. are not in the flesh but in the Spirit, if the Spirit of God dwells in you." Romans 8:9
"Those who live according to the flesh set their minds on the things of the flesh, but those who live according to the Spirit set their minds on the things of the Spirit." Romans 8:5

9. Is it possible for believers to disobey the Holy Spirit and lose the blessing and joy of living for Christ?

Yes, at least temporarily. When we deliberately choose to sin, we grieve the Holy Spirit and lose the peace and joy he gives us when we obey him. But if we have truly been born again, the Spirit will bring us back to the way of life after we have wandered away from it.

Scripture References
"Do not grieve the Holy Spirit of God, by whom you were sealed for the day of redemption."
Ephesians 4:30
"Do not quench the Spirit." Thessalonians 5:19
The apostle Paul wrote concerning a former fellow worker,
"Demas, in love with this present world, has deserted me." 2 Timothy 4:10
The apostle Peter said to Ananias who had lied about a serious matter: *"Why is it that you have contrived this deed in your heart? You have not lied to man, but to God." Acts 5:4-5*

10. How does the Holy Spirit help us in our prayer life?

The Holy Spirit not only helps us to pray but he also prays for us.

Scripture References
"The Spirit helps us in our weakness. For we do not know what to pray for as we ought, but the Spirit himself intercedes for us. .. And he who searches hearts knows what is the mind of the Spirit, because the Spirit intercedes for the saints according to the will of God." Romans 8:26-27
"Praying at all times in the Spirit, with all prayer and supplication." Ephesians 6:18

11. What are some of the spiritual gifts which the Holy Spirit gives to believers?

The Holy Spirit gives a wonderful variety of gifts to believers. He distributes these gifts to believers in a way and at a time that he himself chooses.

Scripture Reference
"There are varieties of gifts, but the same Spirit.. .. To one is given through the Spirit the utterance of wisdom, and to another the utterance of knowledge. .. to another faith. .. to another gifts of healing. .. to another the working of miracles. .. to another prophecy. .. to another the ability to distinguish between spirits . .. to another various kinds of tongues, to another the interpretation of tongues. All these are empowered by one and the same Spirit, who apportions to each one individually as he wills." 1 Corinthians 12:4-11

12. Is the Holy Spirit concerned about the unity of believers?

Very definitely. The unity of the church is of great importance for the spiritual growth of believers and also for their witness to the unbelieving world.

Scripture References

"(Be) eager to maintain the unity of the Spirit in the bond of peace. .. until we all attain to the unity of the faith. .. and mature manhood." Ephesians 4:3, 13

Jesus prayed: *"[May they] all be one, just as you, Father, are in me, and I in you, that they also may be in us, so that the world may believe that you have sent me.. .. I in them and you in me, that they may become perfectly one, so that the world may know that you sent me and loved them even as you loved me.'" John 17:21, 23*

13. Why should we always follow the leading of the Holy Spirit and use our bodies to honor and glorify God?

Our bodies are a temple of the Holy Spirit who lives within us. We are not our own masters. We belong to God!

Scripture References
"Do you not know that you are God's temple and that God's Spirit dwells in you?" 1 Corinthians 3:16
"We are the temple of the living God." 2 Corinthians 6:16
"Do you not know that your body is a temple of the Holy Spirit within you whom you have from God? You are not your own, for you were bought with a price. So glorify God in your body. 1 Corinthians 6:19-20

14. What promise is given to believers concerning the future resurrection of their bodies?

When Jesus returns to earth again, our earthly bodies will be raised as new glorious bodies that will never die.

Scripture References
"And if the Spirit of him who raised Jesus from the dead dwells in you, he who raised Christ from the dead will also give life to your mortal bodies through his Spirit who dwells in you." Romans 8:11
"When the perishable puts on the imperishable, and the mortal puts on immortality, then shall come to pass the saying that is written: 'Death is swallowed up in victory.'" 1 Corinthians 15:54

15. Can we be sure that we are truly saved?

Yes. When we trust in Jesus as our Savior and seek to follow the leading of the Holy Spirit, the Spirit assures us that we are children of God.

Scripture References
"All who are led by the Spirit of God are sons of God.. .. The Spirit himself bears witness with our spirit that we are children of God." Romans 8:14-16
"I write these things to you who believe in the name of the Son of God that you may know that have eternal life." 1 John 5:13

Exploring Further

1. Who is the Holy Spirit?

The Holy Spirit is God just as the Father is God and the Son is God. The Holy Spirit is referred to as the "third person" of the Holy Trinity. When we speak of three "persons," the word "persons" does not refer to three independent beings who exist totally independent from each other. There is only one true God. Neither the Father nor the Son nor the Holy Spirit existed before the others and none has more power or honor than another. However, within the divine Trinity, different "activities" are often associated with one or another of the three "persons." For example, the Father sent the Son into the world. The Son came to earth and took on human form. The Holy Spirit gave life to the baby Jesus in the womb of Mary and also gives new spiritual birth to people and sanctifies them. It is impossible for us to fully understand the one eternal God, but we humbly accept what the Bible teaches us about him.

2. Since the Bible never uses the word "Trinity," why do Christians use that word when referring to God?

The word "Trinity" essentially means "three (tri) in one (unity)." The Bible clearly and repeatedly teaches that there is only one true God. However, it also clearly teaches that the Father is God, the Son is God, and the Holy Spirit is God. The word "Trinity" in this context therefore refers to the "unity" of the three persons referred to in the Bible as Father, Son, and Holy Spirit. People have tried to find some analogies or parallels to this profound concept of "three-in-one" in the world of nature, but all analogies are insufficient to describe the unique oneness of God. Though many books have been written about God and many sermons have been preached about him, we will always have to acknowledge that as human beings it is impossible for us to fully understand everything God has revealed to us about himself in the Bible. At the same time, we may confidently say and believe that there is only true God who exists eternally as Father, Son, and Holy Spirit.

3. What difference would it make if we believed that the Holy Spirit was simply some kind of divine "influence" rather than a "Person?"

First of all, we would be denying many of the things that the Bible teaches us about the Holy Spirit. If the Spirit of God was not truly personal, we would not be able to have fellowship with him, pray to him, or ask him for guidance, comfort, courage, wisdom, and strength. Also, the Holy Spirit could not pray for us. We cannot pray to an influence and an "influence" cannot pray for us! Further, if the Holy Spirit is only an influence of some kind, it would be rather meaningless for us to baptize believers in the name of the Father and the Son and an influence. Also, Paul's final greetings in 2 Corinthians 13:14 would seem very strange, since it refers to the grace of Jesus, the love of God, and the fellowship of the Holy Spirit. The Holy Spirit is definitely a very strong "influence" in our lives, but he is able to influence our lives in so many positive ways precisely because he is both divine and personal.

4. According to the Bible, what are some of the things that the Holy Spirit does?

The Bible states that the Holy Spirit speaks, teaches, loves, comforts, enlightens, understands, communicates, leads, guides, unites believers, gives spiritual gifts to believers, and is grieved when we sin. The Holy Spirit was an agent of creation in the beginning and continues to create new spiritual life in the hearts of believers. He prays for us, cares about us, knows our needs, responds to our prayers, gives us spiritual gifts, comforts us, and works in our hearts and lives to make us more like Christ. The Holy Spirit also empowered Jesus for his ministry on earth. There are very many passages in the Bible that tell us about the work and ministry of the Holy Spirit in both Old Testament and New Testament times. Among them are the following: Genesis 1:2; Psalm 104:30; Matthew 1:18, 20; Matthew 3:13-17; John 14:16-17; 15:26; 16:5-11; Acts 2:1-6; Romans 8:1-11, 26-27; 1 Corinthians 6:19-20; 12:1-13; Galatians 5:16-25; Ephesians 4:3-4.

5. How can we receive the fullness of the Spirit's blessings in our lives?

We receive the Holy Spirit as a gift of grace and not because of our personal goodness or spiritual activities. However, we may (and should) pray for the Holy Spirit to continue to work in our lives, keep us from sin, help us to resist and overcome temptation, lead us to repentance, strengthen our faith, increase our understanding, and enable us to be more like Christ. If we choose to resist the work of the Spirit in our lives through deliberate disobedience or indifference or selfish living, we will not enjoy the special gifts of the Spirit or experience his life-changing power. God often responds to our earnest prayers by giving us special spiritual blessings, so we should continue to pray that we will be filled with the power and presence of the Holy Spirit so that we may continually live in a way that honors and glorifies him.

6. What are some of the special gifts that the Holy Spirit gives to believers?

1 Corinthians 12 gives us a list of many of the special gifts of the Spirit. Some people are given special wisdom to know and understand the Scriptures and to discern the will of God. They may also have wisdom to know how to respond to a specific need or to a difficult or challenging situation. Some are given a special knowledge of another person's needs, concerns, and problems and even their thoughts. They may also have knowledge of a situation far removed from where they are at the moment and know how best to respond to that situation. Others are given the gift of exceptional faith to deal with a special need or concern.

Others are given the ability to perform healing miracles and, in some cases, even to raise the dead. Others are able to work miracles of one kind or another, foretell the future, or discern the truth or falsehood of what others are saying or teaching. Some are able to speak (at least temporarily) in languages which they have not studied or learned. Others are able to interpret things which others are saying in a language they have not learned. Some also seem to be given the gifts of compassion and love and patience and generosity, though these are not specifically mentioned in 1 Corinthians 12.

Believers who place a strong emphasis on these special gifts are sometimes referred to as Pentecostals, since the Holy Spirit came upon the church on the day of Pentecost in power and with special gifts of various kinds. One does not have to be a member of a Pentecostal church, however, in order to receive these gifts or to believe that the Holy Spirit still gives very special gifts and powers to believers today.

7. Do all Christians have the same spiritual gifts? Will the Holy Spirit give us whatever special gifts we ask for?

The answer to both questions is NO. The Holy Spirit does not give the same gifts to everyone. In 1 Corinthians 12:11, Paul writes that the Spirit gives gifts to each one *"as he determines"* and not as *we* request. He re-emphasizes that again in verses 27-30 of this chapter where he indicates that not all are teachers, not all work miracles, not all have gifts of healing, and not all speak in tongues or interpret them. At the same time, he urges his readers to *"eagerly desire the greater gifts."* It is interesting, however, that Paul does not indicate which of these gifts might be "greater." Earlier in the chapter he emphasizes that the church needs all the gifts and that we should not disparage any of the gifts, even though they might seem to be "less important." (See his discussion of this subject in 1 Corinthians 12:12-26.) Believers should be very careful not to esteem certain gifts above others in such a way that people exalt some believers over others because of the specific gift(s) they have received.

8. Galatians 5:22-23 refer to the "fruit" of the Spirit. What "fruit" is referred to in this passage? Do all faithful believers bear the same fruit?

In Galatians 5:22-23 we read that *"The fruit of the Spirit is love, joy, peace, patience, kindness, goodness, faithfulness, gentleness, self-control."* Paul mentions these specific things as important examples of the "fruit" produced by the Holy Spirit in the lives of Jesus' followers. However, this should not be considered a complete or exhaustive list. For example, one could also mention such other "fruit" produced by the Spirit as holiness, generosity, thoughtfulness, and perseverance.

Regrettably, not all believers exhibit all the fruit mentioned in Galatians 5:23. Some, for example, may demonstrate much love and kindness in their lives, though they may not always be patient or joyful. Others may be patient and joyful but still have some significant moral weaknesses in their lives. The reason for this lack of fruit in our lives is because of our sinful nature and our willful pursuit of certain things which do not please God. Regrettably, no one is perfect and no one is totally free from sin in his life. However, if there is little or no spiritual "fruit" in a person's life, there is good reason to question whether Christ truly lives in that person's heart.

9. Ephesians 4:3 and 4:12-13 refer to the unity of the Spirit. Is the church of Christ united today? If it is, how does that unity manifest itself? If it is not, how should we pursue the unity that these passages refer to?

All born-again believers, no matter whether they are Jews or Gentiles, men or women, young or old, educated or uneducated, are united together as one in Christ Jesus. Christ is the sole Head of this church and all believers are equally members of it. They have the same spiritual life, enjoy the same blessings of salvation, and receive the same promises from God. In that sense the church of Christ is definitely united.

Christians manifest this unity in Christ in various ways. One very significant way is by confessing the same basic truths—such as those in the Apostles Creed and other historic Christian creeds. Sincere Christians all recognize and acknowledge that they have been saved through their faith in Jesus who gave his life for them. They also share a heartfelt conviction that they will spend eternity with each other in joy and glory in the presence of their Lord and Savior.

Further, Christians of different denominations worship together on special occasions and also join with other believers in working together to minister to the poor and needy in the name of Christ. They also share in such activities as Scripture translation, distribution of the Scriptures, and in promoting the Bible's teachings regarding moral or social issues. Examples of this are found in the efforts to promote pro-life activities or to promote Biblical teachings on marriage, drug use, sexuality and other moral issues.

However, the church is regrettably and obviously very divided into a great number of denominations throughout the world. Starting a new denomination is often very easy. Many times a person with special gifts of speaking, fund raising or persuasion will begin his "own" church and gain a number of followers who appreciate this person's gifts or abilities. As a result, the number of "denominations" in the world is distressingly large. In many instances, members of different denominations agree on many basic issues, but they disagree on certain practices or beliefs or organizational matters. When that happens, it makes it more difficult to convince non-believers that the church is truly united as one in Christ.

To promote the kind of unity Ephesians refers to, Christians should pray for one another, encourage each other, work together in sharing the Gospel in various meaningful ways, support non-denominational organizations that promote Bible translation and Bible distribution, join together in helping to meet the needs of the poor and others in the name of Christ, and unite with others in promoting Biblical teachings on social and moral issues where they are in agreement. And, without giving up their own understanding of the Scriptures, they should seek to understand the views of others so that they can deal with them patiently, lovingly, and fairly.

10. What are some of the practical implications of the fact that the Holy Spirit lives within us?

Students will probably suggest a variety of meaningful things here based on their own understanding of the Scriptures or on their own personal experience. Among the things which may be mentioned here are the following. The presence of the Holy Spirit in our lives should provide us with courage, comfort, wisdom, confidence, spiritual boldness and a strong desire to witness to others about Jesus. The indwelling Holy Spirit will also help us to remember that we should always use our bodies, our minds, and our personal resources in ways which please and honor our Lord. Through the presence and the power of the Holy Spirit we will also be able to grow in grace, resist and overcome temptation, be sensitive to the needs of others, and exhibit the fruit of the Spirit in our lives. We do not have to face life's trials, problems, challenges, or difficulties in our own strength, but we can depend on the One who dwells within us who is all-knowing and all-powerful. What a tremendous blessing it is to be filled with the Spirit as we presently live our lives on this earth and as we prepare for and anticipate our eternal life with Christ in glory.

Lesson Seven: Christian Living

Introduction

Many people are eager to accept the salvation that Jesus gives. However, they often have questions about *living* as a Christian. Some wonder whether they will be *able* to live a Christian life. Others aren't sure that they are *willing* to do all that Jesus might ask of them. Still others are afraid that Christianity will take all the fun out of their lives.

What does it mean to live as a Christian? Can anyone really live a life that is pleasing to God? Does Christianity really take all the fun and joy out of life?

Before trying to answer those questions, it is important for us to reflect on Jesus' own life. Jesus' life was never easy! He had no home of his own, he had very few personal possessions, and he likely had no personal means of transportation (such as a donkey on which to ride). He was often rejected, misunderstood, ridiculed, falsely accused, and mistreated. Even though he performed many wonderful miracles of healing, fed multitudes of people when they were hungry, showed love and compassion to the poor, showed grace to people that others ignored and forgave people whom others condemned, there were still many people who hated and despised him and tried to find fault with him. Most of the members of his own family misunderstood him at first. One of his closest followers denied him. Another betrayed him. And the rest deserted him when he was confronted by a mob of people in the middle of the night.

If we want to be true followers of Jesus, therefore, we should not expect that our lives will always be easy or pleasant or free from pain. Our blessings will be greater than any we have ever had before, but our challenges and trials may be greater, too. But whatever our circumstances may be—times of exceptional joy or times of suffering and sorrow, Jesus has promised that he will never leave us or forsake us. He will graciously forgive us when we fail, uphold us when we are weak, comfort us when we are rejected or hurt, and continue to shower us with his mercy, grace, and love.

Read thoughtfully and humbly what the Bible says about both the challenges and the blessings of living as a follower of Jesus.

1. What challenge does Jesus give to those who want to follow him?

Jesus challenges us to give up everything for him—even our lives, if necessary.

Scripture References

Jesus said: *"'If anyone would come after me, let him deny himself and take up his cross and follow me. For whoever would save his life will lose it, but whoever loses his life for my sake and the gospel's will save it.'" Mark 8:34-35*
"'Whoever who does not bear his own cross and come after me cannot be my disciple.'" Luke 14:27
"'Whoever loves father or mother more than me is not worthy of me, and whoever loves son or daughter more than me is not worthy of me. And whoever does not take his cross and follow me is not worthy of me.'" Matthew 10:37-38

2. What will motivate us to live for Christ?

We can never repay Jesus for all that he has done for us, but when we humbly reflect on his great love and his incredible sacrifice, we should gratefully seek to live every moment in a way that pleases him. When we think about the wonderful home he is preparing for us in glory, it should not be difficult to give up any earthly treasure or pleasure which does not please him or honor him. Jesus is truly a "priceless treasure" and nothing on earth can compare with him. If we truly love him with all our heart, we will not get swept away with the concerns and pleasures of this world.

Scripture References

Jesus said: *"If anyone loves me, he will keep my word, and my Father will love him, and we will come to him and make our home with him." John 14:23*

"I appeal to you therefore, brothers, by the mercies of God, to present your bodies as a living sacrifice, holy and acceptable to God.. .. Do not be conformed to this world, but be transformed by the renewal of your mind, that by testing you may discern what is the will of God, what is good and acceptable and perfect." Romans 12:1-2

3. Who makes it possible for us to live a Christian life?

God himself does. We are not able to live a consistent Christian life on our own—and, thankfully, we do not have to. God dwells within us through the Holy Spirit who empowers us to live the kind of life that pleases him.

Scripture References
"It is God who works in you, both to will and to work for his good pleasure." Philippians 2:13
"Walk by the Spirit, and you will not gratify the desires of the flesh." Galatians 5:16
"May the God of peace. .. equip you with everything good that you may do his will, working in us that which is pleasing in his sight, through Jesus Christ, to whom be glory forever and ever. Amen." Hebrews 13:20-21

4. How can we show that God is truly at work in our lives?

We should live in such a way that others can see our changed lives. If there is no significant difference between our lives and the lives of those who are not believers, our witness will likely have very little effect. People are much more impressed by how we live than by what we say. If they are able to see that we have truly been transformed by God's grace and power, they will often be eager to know what has happened in our lives.

Scripture References

Paul wrote: *"Christ Jesus came into the world to save sinners—of whom I am the foremost. But I received mercy for this reason, that in me, as the foremost, Jesus Christ might display his perfect patience as an example to those who were to believe in him for eternal life." 1 Timothy 1:15-16*

"The grace of God. .. [trains us] to renounce ungodliness and worldly passions, and to live self-controlled, upright, and godly lives in the present age. .. [Jesus Christ] gave himself for us to redeem us from all lawlessness and to purify for himself a people for his own possession who are zealous for good works." Titus 2:11-12, 14

"We ourselves were once foolish, disobedient, led astray, slaves to various passions and pleasures.. . But when the goodness and loving kindness of God our Savior appeared, he saved us, not because of works done by us in righteousness, but according to his own mercy, by the washing of regeneration and renewal of the Holy Spirit. I [Paul] want you to insist on these things, so that those who have believed in God may be careful. .. to devote themselves to good works." Titus 3:3-5,8

5. Is it important for Christians to show genuine love to one another?

Yes. The two greatest commandments in both the Old Testament and the New Testament are these: Love God above all and love others as yourselves (Matthew 22:37-40). As Jesus himself said, others will know that you are his disciple if you have genuine love for others—even for people who might be considered unlovable. Since God loved us when we ourselves were unlovable, our lives demonstrate what God can do in any life that is committed to him.

Scripture References
"Beloved, if God so loved us, we also ought to love one another.. .. if we love one another, God abides in us and his love is perfected in us." 1 John 4:11-12

Jesus said: *"'By this all people will know that you are my disciples, if you have love for one another.'"John 13:35*

"Let love be genuine. Abhor what is evil; hold fast to what is good. Love one another with brotherly affection. Outdo one another in showing honor." Romans 12:9-10

6. What is Christian love like?

Genuine Christian love is self-giving, consistent, helpful, thoughtful, and often sacrificial. It is primarily "love in action" rather than simply love in words or feelings. It is basically a reflection of Christ's love *for* us and *within* us. Without Christ's love and the power of the Holy Spirit within us, it would impossible for us to love others in the way that God commands and which the Bible describes.

Scripture References
"'Greater love has no one than this that someone lays down his life for his friends.'" John 15:13
"Love does no wrong to a neighbor." Romans 13:10
"Love covers a multitude of sins." 1 Peter 4:8
"Love is patient and kind; love does not envy or boast; it is not arrogant or rude. It does not insist on its own way; it is not irritable or resentful; it does not rejoice at wrongdoing, but rejoices with the truth. Love bears all things, believes all things, hopes all things, endures all things. Love never ends. As for prophecies, they will pass away; as for tongues, they will cease; as for knowledge, it will pass away." 1 Corinthians 13:4-8

7. What does the Bible teach about worldliness?

"Worldliness" is thinking and living according to the standards and desires of the sinful and unbelieving world rather than living according to the teachings of the Word of God. Those who live by the world's goals and standards are not living in a way that pleases God. Friendship with the world makes a person an enemy of God.

Scripture References
"Do not love the world or the things in the world. If anyone loves the world, the love of the Father is not in him. For all that is in

the world—the desires of the flesh and the desires of the eyes and pride in possessions—is not from the Father but is from the world." 1 John 2:15-16

"The grace of God. .. [trains]us to renounce ungodliness and worldly passions, and to live self-controlled, upright, and godly lives in the present age." Titus 2:11-12

"Do you not know that friendship with the world is enmity with God? Therefore whoever wishes to be a friend of the world makes himself an enemy of God." James 4:4

8. What are some of the specific sins which the Bible warns against?

The Bible warns against sins of every kind—sins of thought, word or deed. Some of the specific sins listed in the New Testament include lying, stealing, fighting, bad language, immorality, drunkenness, uncontrolled anger, greed, bitterness. .. and many others.

Scripture References

"Therefore, having put away falsehood, let each one of you speak the truth with his neighbor, for we are members one of another.. .. Do not let the sun go down on your anger and give no opportunity to the devil. Let the thief no longer steal.. .. Let no corrupting talk come out of your mouths, but only such as is good for building up.. .. Do not grieve the Holy Spirit of God. Let all bitterness and wrath and anger and clamor and slander be put away from you.. . .Sexual immorality and all impurity or covetousness must not even be named among you, as is proper among saints. Let there be no filthiness nor foolish talk nor crude joking, which are out of place. For you may be sure of this, that everyone who is sexually immoral or impure, or who is covetous (that is, an idolater), has no inheritance in the kingdom of Christ and God.. .. Do not be foolish but understand what the will of the Lord is. And do not get drunk with wine, for that is debauchery, but be filled with the Spirit." Ephesians 4:25-31; 5:3-5, 17-18

"In the last days. .. people will be lovers of self, lovers of money, proud, arrogant, abusive, disobedient to their parents, ungrateful, unholy, heartless, unappeasable, slanderous, without self-control,

brutal, not loving good, treacherous, reckless, swollen with deceit, lovers of pleasure rather than lovers of God, having the appearance of godliness, but denying its power. Avoid such people." 2 Timothy 3:1-5

9. Is it possible for us to overcome temptation and live a holy life?

Yes. God provides a way out of each trial and temptation if we sincerely look for it and desire it. But if we do not sincerely look for a way out of the temptation, we very likely will not find it.

Scripture References

"No temptation has overtaken you that is not common to man. God is faithful, and he will not let you be tempted beyond your ability, but with the temptation, he will also provide the way of escape, that you may be able to endure it." 1 Corinthians 10:13
"Our Lord Jesus Christ. .. will sustain you to the end, guiltless in the day of our Lord Jesus Christ. God is faithful, by whom you were called into the fellowship of his Son, Jesus Christ our Lord." 1 Corinthians 1:7-9
"To him who is able to keep you from stumbling and to present you blameless before the presence of his glory with great joy, to the only God our Savior. .. be glory before all time and now and forever. Amen." Jude 24-25

10. Is God willing to forgive us if we fall into sin even after confessing Christ?

Yes. God will graciously forgive us if we sincerely confess our sins and humbly ask him to forgive us. However, that does not mean that we should take our sins lightly. God is indeed gracious and merciful, but our sins and failures grieve the Holy Spirit who lives within us. Our sins also dishonor the name of God and may also diminish the effectiveness of our personal testimony.

Scripture References

"If we confess our sins, he is faithful and just to forgive us our sins and to cleanse us from all unrighteousness." 1 John 1:9

"Whoever conceals his transgressions will not prosper, but he who confesses and forsakes them will obtain mercy." Proverbs 28:13

"I acknowledged my sin to you, and I did not cover my iniquity. I said, 'I will confess my transgressions to the LORD,' and you forgave the iniquity of my sin." Psalm 32:5

11. How can we help each other live a Christian life?

We should worship together, encourage one another, pray for each other, and be careful never to tempt one another or lead one another into sin.

Scripture References

"Let us consider how to stir up one another to love and good deeds, not neglecting to meet together, as is the habit of some, but encouraging one another, and all the more as you see the Day drawing near." Hebrews 10:24-25

"Keep alert with all perseverance, making supplication for all the saints [believers]." Ephesians 6:18

"Take care that this right of yours does not somehow become a stumbling block to the weak." 1 Corinthians 8:9

"Finally, all of you, have unity of mind, sympathy, brotherly love, a tender heart, and a humble mind. Do not repay evil for evil or reviling for reviling, but on the contrary, bless, for to this you were called, that you may obtain a blessing." 1 Peter 3:8-9

12. What attitude should we have toward money and possessions?

It is a wonderful blessing to have sufficient funds and resources for daily living. We should be very careful, however, not to put too much emphasis on material things or value them too highly. We should be grateful for all that the Lord entrusts to us, be content with what we have, and not be envious of others who have more than we do. We should also recognize that we are only stewards of the things the Lord has entrusted to us.

Everything we call our own really belongs to him. When possible, we should also use our possessions to serve the poor and the homeless in the name of the Lord so that he is glorified while we help to meet the needs of others. And we should also use our financial resources to help spread the good news of the Gospel around the world.

Scripture References
"'Be on your guard against all covetousness, for one's life does not consist in the abundance of possessions." Luke 12:15
"Keep your life free from love of money, and be content with what you have." Hebrews 13:5
"If anyone has the world's goods and sees his brother in need, yet closes his heart against him, how does God's love abide in him?" 1 John 3:17
"We brought nothing into the world, and we cannot take anything out of the world. But if we have food and clothing, with these we will be content. But those who desire to be rich fall into temptation, into a snare.. .. For the love of money is a root of all kinds of evils. It is through this craving that some have wandered away from the faith and pierced themselves with many pangs." 1 Timothy 6:7-10

13. What does the Bible teach about giving?

We should give generously, regularly, and cheerfully. A special object of our giving should be believers who are in need, though we should also remember the needs of others.

Scripture References
"As we have opportunity, let us do good to everyone, and especially to those who are of the household of faith." Galatians 6:10
"As you excel in everything. .. see that you excel in this act of grace also." 2 Corinthians 8:7
"Each one must give as he has decided in his heart, not reluctantly or under compulsion, for God loves a cheerful giver." 2 Corinthians 9:7

14. What are the results of generous and cheerful giving?

Those who give are blessed, the needs of others are met, and God is honored and praised.

Scripture References
"Whoever has a bountiful eye will be blessed, for he shares his bread with the poor." Proverbs 22:9
"Whoever sows sparingly will also reap sparingly, and whoever sows bountifully will also reap bountifully." 2 Corinthians 9:6
"The ministry of this service is not only supplying the needs of the saints [believers] but is also overflowing in many thanksgivings to God." 2 Corinthians 9:12

15. Doesn't living as a Christian take the fun and joy out of life?

Not at all. Living as an obedient Christian in a non-Christian world can certainly be challenging and difficult at times. But the blessings of living for Christ far outweigh any difficulties involved. Not only has Jesus promised that we will live with him forever in glory, but he also promised that our Father in heaven will graciously meet all our needs in our present life. In fact, God often gives us material and physical blessings which go far beyond what we actually need. In addition, he also gives us gifts of love and joy and peace which the world can never give. Even though we may experience trials or difficulties in this life because we are Christians, God promises that whatever suffering and difficulties we experience as believers will eventually turn out for our spiritual and eternal good.

Scripture References
"God is able to make all grace abound to you, so that having all sufficiency in all things at all times, you may abound in every good work." 2 Corinthians 9:8
"Rejoice in the Lord always. .. and the peace of God, which surpasses all understanding, will guard your hearts and your minds in Christ Jesus." Philippians 4:4-7
"Though you have not seen him [Jesus], you love him. Though you do not now see him, you

believe in him and rejoice with joy that is inexpressible and filled with glory." 1 Peter 1:8
"According to his great mercy he [God] has caused us to be born again to a living hope. . to an inheritance that is imperishable, undefiled, and unfading, kept in heaven for you." 1 Peter 1: 3-4
"This slight and momentary affliction is preparing for us an eternal weight of glory beyond all comparison." 2 Corinthians 4:17

16. Should believers witness to unbelievers about Jesus Christ?

Definitely. We should be prepared to witness to others whenever possible. However, we should also be wise and humble as we talk to people who are not yet believers. If we have an attitude of superiority when we talk to them, this will often turn them away from both us and Christ. Also, we must be very careful to make sure that our lives reflect what we profess. If our lives are not consistent with our testimony, our witnessing will usually produce little fruit. We must continually seek to live in the love of Jesus and in the power of the Holy Spirit so that our witness will be meaningful and effective.

Scripture References
"Always be prepared to make a defense to anyone who asks you for a reason for the hope that is in you; yet do it with gentleness and respect." 1 Peter 3:15
"Conduct yourselves wisely toward outsiders; making the best use of the time. Let your speech always be gracious, seasoned with salt, so that you may know how you ought to answer each person." Colossians 4:5-6
The apostle Paul wrote: *"I have become all things to all people, that by all possible means I might save some." 1 Corinthians 9:22*
"Whoever brings back a sinner from his wandering will save his soul from death and will cover a multitude of sins." James 5:20

17. Where can we get the wisdom and power we need to witness effectively to others?

We can receive all the wisdom and power we need from the Holy Spirit.

Scripture References
Jesus said: *"'You will receive power when the Holy Spirit has come up on you, and you will be my witnesses. .. to the ends of the earth.'" Acts 1:8*

Jesus said: *"'The Helper, the Holy Spirit, whom the Father will send in my name, he will teach you all things and bring to your remembrance all that I have said to you.'" John 14:26*
Jesus said: *"'When the Spirit of truth, comes, he will guide you into all the truth.'" John 16:13*

18. What general guidelines should we follow as we seek to live a Christian life?

We should always seek to follow the leading of the Holy Spirit, live lives of thankfulness, do all things in the name of Jesus, and seek to do all things to the glory of God.

Scripture References
"Whether you eat or drink, or whatever you do, do it all for the glory of God." 1 Corinthians 10:31
"Walk by the Spirit, and you will not gratify the desires of the flesh." Galatians 5:16
"Whatever you do, in word or deed, do everything in the name of the Lord Jesus, giving thanks to God the Father through him." Colossians 3:17
"As each has received a gift, use it to serve one another, as good stewards of God's varied grace: whoever speaks, as one who speaks oracles of God; whoever serves, as one who serves by the strength that God supplies—in order that in everything God may be glorified through Jesus Christ. To him belong glory and dominion forever and ever. Amen." 1 Peter 4:10-11

Exploring Further

1. Since we are saved by grace and not by our works, what difference does it make how we live?

There are several things that are important to remember in this regard. (a) If we are truly saved, we will want to live in a way that honors and glorifies our Savior. If we are careless about the way we live, we clearly demonstrate that Christ does not really live within us. And if Christ does not live within us, we are not truly saved. (b) God has saved us not only for our own benefit but also so that we may live for his glory and be a blessing to others. Ephesians 2:10 tells us that God has "prepared" good works for us to do, and in gratitude, humility, and thankfulness we will sincerely want to do these works. (c) If we are not living in a way that honors God and blesses others, our lives will have a negative impact rather than a positive one. (d) There will be a judgment day in which God will call us to give an account for all that we have done. Those who have sincerely sought to please him will be richly rewarded for the things they have done in the name and in the power of the Lord. Those who have not honored and served the Lord will find that their works were totally worthless. (Read Matthew 25:31-46; 2 Corinthians 5:9-10; Matthew 12:36; 1 Peter 1:17; 1 Peter 4:5; 1 Thessalonians 4:1; Romans 14:12; Hebrews 13:16; 1 Corinthians 3:10-15.)

2. If we do not give up everything for Jesus (Mark 8:34-35), does that mean we are not really Christians?

Not necessarily. In some places, Christians do give up everything or almost everything for the sake of Jesus because they live in an area where Christians are persecuted for their faith. Other believers live in areas and under circumstances where the practice of their faith actually results in greater material benefits. People trust them to be honest, hard-working, dependable, and competent and reward them for their integrity. These believers seem to give up very little for the sake of Jesus.

Are these people less honorable, less faithful, and less "Christian" than other believers whose lives are so very difficult?

The key to answering this question would seem to be the willingness of people to give up anything and everything that would stand in the way of living as a believer who honors Christ in everything. All believers should evaluate their lives to make sure that they are using all their gifts and abilities and possessions in the service of Christ without focusing too much on material things or personal benefits. We should all be careful not to judge others too quickly without knowing their hearts and motives. Having riches is not wrong for a Christian, but the "love of money" is clearly a source of many evils in our world. See 1 Timothy 6:6-10; Matthew 6:19-20; Luke 12:33; Philippians 3:8; Ecclesiastes 2:26; James 2:5.

Students will probably have some very helpful and important observations here, based partly on the Scriptures and partly on their own personal experience or the experience of other Christians.

3. **If others cannot see in our daily walk that we are truly followers of Christ, does that mean that we probably are not true Christians—no matter what we say or believe?**

In most situations a true believer will demonstrate his faith by his life. If he doesn't, there is probably something wrong in his life. There may be times, of course, when believers are very careful about what they say and do since they know others are watching them in order to find grounds for "punishing" them or "persecuting" them. These believers do not deny their faith or live a careless or thoughtless life. They simply do not have the freedom that Christians in other lands have to speak about Jesus or the Bible or their faith.

All believers should also remember, however, that there may be some people who are looking at them to see whether their Christian faith really does make a meaningful difference in their lives. If it doesn't, the non-believers who are watching them may not want to have anything to do with Christianity. However, if believers quietly and consistently demonstrate love, genuine concern for others, patience, holiness, thoughtfulness, consistency, and other positive virtues, people who are carefully watching them may well want to learn more about their faith and the God they worship.

We should never be ashamed of our faith, but we should also be wise as we seek to live out our faith in a way that most honors and pleases God and also blesses others. Read the following passages from the New Testament. Luke 9:23-26; Mark 8:38; Matthew 28:19-20; John 15:27; Acts 1:8; 5:20; 22:15; Titus 2:15; 2 Timothy 1:8; 1 Peter 4:16.

4. **What does Paul teach about Christian love in 1 Corinthians 13?**

Though the Bible discusses Christian love in various places, 1 Corinthians 13 is widely recognized as the most important teaching in the entire Bible on this subject. This chapter can be profitably read aloud and discussed with many specific illustrations that students have personally experienced or which they have heard about. Among other specific questions which might be discussed here are the following: (1) Do most Christians exhibit the kind of love described in this chapter? (2) How does a person "acquire" this kind of love? Is this something we have to "work at" or do we simply pray and ask God for it? (3) Can we learn from others how to acquire and exhibit Christian love? (4)What should we do if we are members of a church which is definitely not known for its Christian love? (5) Should Christians show the kind of love discussed in this chapter only to other Christians, or should they show love also to those who are not Christians and may even hate or oppress them?

5. **What is meant by "worldliness"? Is it possible to be a "worldly Christian"?**

Worldliness can be described as thinking and living according to the standards, goals and desires of people who do not know

Christ as Lord and Savior. If that description is correct, then it really is not possible to be a "worldly Christian." It is regrettably true, however, that some believers seem to live as "close" to the world as they can without losing their faith. And most believers seem to be tempted at least once in a while to enjoy "worldly pleasures" instead of doing what is most pleasing to God and most beneficial for their personal and spiritual lives. Sincere Christians should always seek to live as close to Christ as they can, learning and doing what is most pleasing to him and seeking to honor him in all the choices they make. Read the following passages which teach us important things about worldliness. Matthew 16:26; Luke 21:34; Romans 12:2; Colossians 3:2; Titus 2:12; James 4:4; 1 John 2:15-17; Ephesians 2:2.

Though believers should not be "worldly" in a negative sense, Christians should definitely be concerned about demonstrating the Lordship of Jesus in every area of their lives. They should not focus only on so-called "spiritual things," but they should also seek to show the importance of their Christian faith in the world of business, government, work, recreation, leisure, industry, the arts and every other area of human activity. Christians should seek to "transform" the world in positive ways without being contaminated by those practices and activities that dishonor the One who is truly Lord of All.

6. **Will the Lord continue to forgive us even if we commit the same sins over and over again?**

Thankfully, YES! God's mercy and grace are far greater than our failures and sins (Psalm 103:2-3, 8-14, 17; Micah 7:18-19; Isaiah 1:18; Ephesians1:7; Matthew 6:14; 1 John 1:9). However, we should never take our sins lightly or think that it doesn't matter very much whether we keep sinning or not. God is grieved by our sins (Ephesians 4:30; Genesis 6:6; Isaiah 63:10) and our sins also diminish the effectiveness of our witness and reduce the joy of our salvation. If there are certain sins or weaknesses that continually gain a victory over us, we should not only pray earnestly to the Lord for deliverance, but we should also seek the help of mature Christians to help us gain a victory over them.

Many believers find that it is very helpful to have one or more mature Christians to whom they are regularly accountable for how they are living—particularly in those areas where they are spiritually and morally weak.

7. **What does 1 Peter 3:8-9 teach us about living a Christian life?**

Peter urges us to live in harmony with other believers and to love them as brothers in Christ. We should be sensitive to the needs of others, and compassionate and humble as we deal with them. We should also be careful not to repay evil for evil but to bless those who curse us or insult us or treat us unkindly. Living as God wants us to live will not only bring a blessing to others but will also result in blessing for ourselves.

It is certainly easier to write these things, however, than to practice them. Peter, at one stage in his life, didn't follow these teachings himself. When he was in the Garden of Gethsemane on the night before Jesus went to the cross, he impetuously took out his sword and cut off the ear of one of the men who had come to arrest Jesus. (And he may have tried to do more than just cut off his ear!) All of us have to make a very special effort to be patient and compassionate and humble as we deal with others. Peter wisely points to Jesus rather than himself when looking for a good example. In 1 Peter 2:20-23 we read: *"If when you do good and suffer for it you endure, this is a gracious thing in the sight of God. For to this you have been called, because Christ also suffered for you, leaving you an example, so that you might follow in his steps... .When he was reviled, he did not revile in return; when he suffered, he did not threaten, but continued entrusting himself to him who judges justly."* In 1 Peter 2:12 he wrote: *"Keep your conduct among the Gentiles honorable, so that when they speak against you as evildoers, they may see your good deeds and glorify God on the day of visitation."*

8. What are some of the things the Bible teaches about money and possessions?

God knows that we all need certain things—such as food, water, clothing and shelter—in order to live a normal life (Matthew 6:31-32). In his kindness, he provides rain from heaven, crops in their season, food and water and many other things to fill our hearts with joy (Acts 14:17). In addition, God often makes it possible for some people to acquire possessions far beyond what they need for daily living. Already in the Old Testament, for example, many of God's faithful followers were blessed with great wealth: Abraham (Genesis 13:2), Isaac (Genesis 26:13-14), Jacob (Genesis 30:43), Job (Job 1:3), David (1 Chronicles 29:28), and Solomon (2 Chronicles 1:15). The problem is not having great possessions but how we look upon them and how we use them. Some people feel that their personal worth is determined by the money or possessions they have. Others begin to take their blessings for granted. They may feel that they deserve their wealth because of their personal skills or all the hard work they have done. Still others feel that they may spend their money as they please (unless it clearly and directly violates one of God's explicit commands).

The Bible therefore clearly and frequently warns against the dangers of putting too much emphasis on material possessions. It also warns against greed, covetousness, selfishness, and pride. See the texts in the Lesson (Luke 12:15; Psalm 62:10; Hebrews 13:5; 1 Timothy 6:10; Luke 16:14; Matthew 19:23; and Matthew 6:31-33). See also such passages as Deuteronomy 8:10-14 and 8:17-18; Mark 4:19; Ecclesiastes 5:10; Psalm 39:6; Psalm 52:7; Luke 12:19-20; James 4:17; and many others.

The Bible teaches us that ALL things ultimately belong to God and that we are simply temporary stewards of the possessions we have. In Old Testament times, God's people were commanded to give at least one-tenth of all their possessions to the Lord (Leviticus 27:30-33; Numbers 18:21; Malachi 3:10) and often were required to give more. In the New Testament believers are not explicitly commanded to give one tenth of their earnings to the Lord, but they are clearly taught that they should give generously, thoughtfully, and freely. Believers may certainly enjoy the blessings God gives them, but they should also recognize that everything they have comes from the Lord and is to be used in ways that most please and honor him and which also bless others in his name. When people give generously and freely and joyfully to others (especially to fellow believers, Galatians 6:10), not only are others blessed, but God is also glorified. See such passages as 2 Corinthians 8:1-23 and 2 Corinthians 9:6-15.

Since our spiritual blessings are much greater after the coming of Christ than they were in Old Testament times, our giving should also be greater (when possible). According to 2 Corinthians 9:7, God loves a cheerful giver. Believers, therefore, should be known for their generous, joyful, thoughtful giving and should never be satisfied with giving as little as they can. Among passages to be read and studied in this connection are the following: Leviticus 25:35; Proverbs 3:9; 11:25; 21:13; 28:27; Deuteronomy 15:4, 7; 16:17; 1 Chronicles 29:9; Isaiah 58:10; Matthew 5:42; Matthew 6:3; Luke 6:38; Luke 12:23; Acts 11:29; 1 Corinthians 4:2; and 1 Peter 4:10.

9. Why should we witness to others about our faith? What should we do in situations where friends or family members absolutely do not want to hear about Jesus?

We should witness to others about our faith because Jesus wants us to and even commands us to do so (Mark 16:15; Luke 24:47; Matthew 24:14; Acts 1:8; Acts 22:15; Titus 2:15; Romans 10:14). However, we should also witness because we want to. If we do not have a desire to share our faith with others, that may indicate (1) that we do not highly value our faith or (2) that we believe others do not need to hear about Jesus or (3) that we believe our testimony will have little or no positive results, or (4) that we are afraid of the reactions of those with whom we share our faith. None of these four possibilities should keep us from witnessing to others, though there may be specific times or situations when it is not wise or desirable to talk to others about

Jesus. For example, a new convert should be wise in choosing the best time and situation in which to witness to family members, friends, or others who might be shocked, grieved or angry when they learn that a trusted friend or loved one has left the cherished faith of the family. Jesus himself told his followers not to throw their *"pearls before pigs"* lest *"they trample them underfoot and turn to attack you"* (Matthew 7:6).

When faced with uncertainty about the best time and way to witness to someone else about Jesus, it is important to pray earnestly that God will open up the right opportunity for us to share our faith when our testimony is most likely to have a positive rather than a negative impact. When giving our testimony, we should also be very careful not to unnecessarily say negative things about other faiths or about persons who hold those faiths. Rather, humbly but clearly we should testify about the things which God has done for us and the joy we have found in loving and serving him. We should, of course, also always be *"prepared to make a defense to anyone who asks you for a reason for the hope that is in you"* (1 Peter 3:15). But, as Peter writes, we should do this *"with gentleness and respect, having a good conscience, so that, when you are slandered, those who revile your good behavior in Christ may be put to shame"* (1 Peter 3: 15-16).

Many students may have some practical experience in this area which could be of much help to fellow students. Be sure to give them the opportunity to share some of their experiences with others.

10. How would you respond to someone who believes that Christianity takes all the fun and joy out of life?

Most students will likely have a variety of responses to this question. Some may acknowledge that they have missed some of the "good times" they had with friends before they were converted. (The reference here is to genuinely good times which a person gave up because he or she no longer wanted to be identified with a certain group of people.) Some may also acknowledge that they lost good jobs because their conscience no longer permitted them to do some of the things they were required to do in their work situations. Others might acknowledge that they lost the loving relationship which they used to have with their families and friends. Still others might indicate that since they became believers they spend more time in studying the Bible, helping others, and pursuing other good things related to their new faith and therefore don't have the time they used to have to pursue some of the fun things they enjoyed doing.

However, those who have genuinely experienced the love and grace of God in new and wonderful ways will be able to testify that what they have given up does not begin to compare with the things they have gained. They have found genuine joy, inner peace, and contentment in the present and hope for the future which they never had before. Because they have been born anew by the Holy Spirit and have been washed clean in the blood of Christ, they are new persons who have something more wonderful and more valuable than anything they have given up. In New Testament times, some believers were persecuted because of their faith but counted it a privilege to suffer for the One who gave his life for their salvation. The apostle Paul considered all the "valuable" things of his previous life to be "rubbish" compared with the new life he found in Jesus (Philippians 3:8). When people truly find new joy and peace in serving Christ, others will soon notice that, so it should not be too difficult for them to demonstrate (even without many words) that their new life provides far more genuine joy and delight than anything they experienced in their life without Christ.

It is also important, however, for believers to be honest and realistic in their testimonies. Paul clearly suffered much more after he became a Christian than he did before he became a Christian and he definitely did not minimize the hardships or difficulties he experienced (2 Corinthians 11:16-29). However, anyone who knew Paul knew that his new life, in spite of these hardships, was definitely a grateful life of joy, peace, thanksgiving, and praise

(Philippians 4:8-9, 11-13). See also Acts 5:41; Hebrews 10:34; and1 Peter 1:8.

Lesson Eight: Prayer

Introduction

One of the great privileges we have as Christians is praying to our Father in heaven. Though he is infinitely greater than we are, we can speak to him at any time about anything. We do not have to make a special reservation to talk to him, we do not have to meet him at a special place, and we do not have to use special words or a special tone of voice when talking to him. All we need is a humble and sincere desire to bring before God the deepest feelings and desires of our hearts. God truly wants us to do that. And he promises to listen when we do!

1. *Why* should we pray?

The Bible frequently encourages us and even commands us to pray. Prayer is the gateway to a close and precious relationship to our Father in heaven.

Scripture References
"The prayer of the upright is acceptable to him." Proverbs 15:8
"Continue steadfastly in prayer, being watchful in it with thanksgiving." Colossians 4:2
"Pray without ceasing." 1 Thessalonians 5:17

2. *How* should we pray?

We should pray in the name of Jesus. Praying in the name of Jesus does not mean that we simply "say" the name of Jesus when we pray. Rather, it means that we pray humbly, confidently and expectantly because of what Jesus has done for us.

Scripture References
Jesus said, *"'Whatever you ask in my name, this I will do, that the Father may be glorified in the Son.'"* John 14:13
Jesus said: *"'Truly, truly I say to you, whatever you ask of the*

Father in my name, he will give it to you. ... Ask, and you will receive, that your joy may be full.'" John 16:23-24
"[Give] thanks always and for everything to God the Father in the name of our Lord Jesus Christ." Ephesians 5:20

3. *What* should we pray about?

We should pray about anything and everything. Though God is infinite and rules over the entire world, he is concerned about even the smallest things in our lives. Even when others might not want to be bothered by our concerns, God is never bothered when we come to him humbly, thoughtfully, and sincerely—no matter what may be on our hearts or minds.

Scripture References
"Do not be anxious about anything, but in everything, by prayer and supplication with thanksgiving let your requests be made known to God." Philippians 4:6
"[Pray] at all times in the Spirit, with all prayer and supplication. To that end keep alert and with all perseverance, making supplication for all the saints [believers]." Ephesians 6:18

4. *When* should we pray?

We may pray at any time. It is often helpful to set aside a special time for prayer each day, but we should not restrict our praying to one particular time. God is willing to hear our prayers at any time of day or night. We may pray while walking, driving, resting, working, playing or at any other time. We may pray publicly, or we may pray silently when others around us are not even aware that we are praying. There is no time or situation when praying is inappropriate.

Scripture References
"All night he [Jesus] continued in prayer to God." Luke 6:12
"And rising very early in the morning, while it was still dark, he [Jesus] departed and went out to a desolate place, and there he prayed." Mark 1:35

"All these with one accord were devoting themselves to prayer."
Acts 1:14
"From the day we heard, we have not ceased to pray for you,
asking that you may be filled with the knowledge of his will in all
spiritual wisdom and understanding." Colossians 1:9

5. *Where* should we pray?

We can pray anywhere and be assured that God hears our
prayers wherever we are. However, it is often desirable to have a
quiet place where we can pray to God without distractions. Jesus
himself went off by himself to quiet places where he could be
alone with his Father in heaven.

Scripture References
"He [Daniel]went to his house where he had windows in his
upper chamber open toward Jerusalem. He got down on his
knees three times a day and prayed and gave thanks before his
God." Daniel 6:10
"Kneeling down on the beach, we prayed." Acts 21:5
"The next day, as they were on their journey and approaching the
city, Peter went up on the housetop about the sixth hour to pray."
Acts 10:9
Jesus said: "'When you pray, go into your room and shut the door*
and pray to your Father who is in secret.'" Matthew 6:6
"He [Jesus] would withdraw to desolate places and pray." Luke
5:16
"He [Jesus] went out to the mountain to pray, and all night he
continued in prayer to God." Luke 6:12

6. Is there a special posture we should have when we pray?

No. We should always be thoughtful, humble, reverent and
sincere when we pray, but there is no special posture required in
order for us to pray in a way that pleases God. We may bow,
kneel, sit, stand, raise our hands, or lie prostrate on the ground
when praying. Many people, however, feel that kneeling in
prayer is a special sign of sincerity and reverence and therefore
usually kneel when they pray in private and often in public as

well.

Scripture References

"I desire then that in every place the men should pray." 1 *Timothy 2:8*

"'I. .. fell upon my knees and spread out my hands to the LORD my God.'" Ezra 9:5-6

"'The tax collector, standing far off, would not even lift up his eyes to heaven, but beat his breast, saying, 'God, be merciful to me, a sinner!'" Luke 18:13

"[The king] bowed his head with his face to the ground, and all Judah and the inhabitants of Jerusalem fell down before the LORD, worshiping the LORD." 2 Chronicles 20:18

"He [Jesus] fell on his face and prayed." Matthew 26:39

"Now as Solomon finished offering all this prayer and plea to the LORD, he arose from before the altar of the LORD, where he had knelt with hands outstretched toward heaven." 1 Kings 8:54

7. Is it appropriate to pray directly to Jesus and to the Holy Spirit as well as to the Father?

Yes. The resurrected and ascended Jesus is reigning as the ruler over the entire universe and is always willing to listen when we pray. The Holy Spirit is our comforter and guide and the one who enables us to live a Christian life. He also hears us when we pray. The Christian church has therefore produced a number of hymns of petition or praise which are specifically directed to Jesus or to the Holy Spirit.

Scripture References

Jesus said, *"'If you ask me anything in my name, I will do it.'" John 14:14*

"As they were stoning Stephen, he called out, 'Lord Jesus, receive my spirit.'" Acts 7:59

"Likewise the Spirit helps us in our weakness. .. the Spirit himself intercedes for us with groanings too deep for words. And he who searches our hearts knows what is the mind of the Spirit, because the Spirit intercedes for the saints [believers] according to the will of God." Romans 8:26-27

8. Does God hear and answer our prayers?

Absolutely! He hears and answers all the prayers of those who pray according to his will. However, he does not always answer our prayers in the way that we personally would choose or desire. At times his response may be "No" and at other times his response may be "Not now." Sometimes he may give us something much better than we had asked for, even though we may not understand immediately why it is better. But whatever his answer might be, we may be confident that our prayers are always heard. (See also questions 10 and 11.)

Scripture References
"This is the confidence that we have toward him, that if we ask anything according to his will he hears us." 1 John 5:14
Jesus said, *"'Ask and it will be given to you; seek, and you will find; knock, and it will be opened to you. For everyone who asks receives, and the one who seeks finds, and to the one who knocks it will be opened.'" Matthew 7:7-8*
Jesus said, *"'If you abide in me, and my words abide in you, ask whatever you wish, and it will be done for you.'" John 15:7*
"Let us then with confidence draw near to the throne of grace, that we may receive mercy and find grace to help in time of need." Hebrews 4:16
"The prayer of a righteous person has great power as it is working." James 5:16

9. Are there any specific examples in the Bible of God's answers to prayer?

Yes. The Bible has many wonderful examples of God's answers to the prayers of his people. Women who were barren gave birth to children, prisoners were set free, battles were won, protection was provided, water and food were given, wisdom was granted, lives were changed, and many other blessings were experienced in answer to prayer.

Scripture References
Hannah said: *"'For this child I prayed, and the LORD has*

granted me my petition that I made to him. Therefore I have lent him to the LORD.'" 1 Samuel 1:27-28

"Elijah was a man with a nature like ours, and he prayed fervently that it might not rain, and for three years and six months it did not rain on the earth. Then he prayed again, and heaven gave rain, and the earth bore its fruit." James 5:17-18

Elijah prayed: "'Answer me, O LORD. .. so these people may know that you, O LORD, are God'.. . Then the fire of the LORD fell and consumed the burnt offering. .. When all the people saw it, they fell on their faces and said, 'The LORD, he is God; the LORD, he is God.'" 1 Kings 18:37-39

An angel came to Zechariah and said: "'Do not be afraid, Zechariah, for your prayer has been heard, and your wife Elizabeth will bear you a son, and you shall call his name John.'" Luke 1:3

"They lifted their voices together to God. .. And when they had prayed, the place where they were gathered was shaken, and they were all filled with the Holy Spirit and continued to speak the word of God with boldness." Acts 4:24, 31

"So Peter was kept in prison, but earnest prayer for him was made to God by the church.. .. an angel of the Lord stood next to him, and a light shone in the cell. He struck Peter on the side and woke him, saying, 'Get up quickly.' And the chains fell off his hands." Acts 12:5,7 (Read the entire story of Peter's miraculous deliverance in Acts 12: 1-17.)

10. **Are there any things that might cause God *not* to answer our prayers in the way we desire?**

Yes. Though God is merciful and gracious, there are certain conditions which must usually be met before our prayers will be answered. Among them are humility, sincerity, obedience, faith, right motives, commitment, and a forgiving spirit. If these and other conditions are not met, our prayers may not be answered in the way we desire.

Scripture References
"'If my people who are called by my name humble themselves, and pray and seek my face and turn from their wicked ways, then

will I hear from heaven and will forgive their sin and heal their land.'" 2 Chronicles 7:14

"If I had cherished iniquity in my heart, the LORD would not have listened." Psalm 66:18

"You ask and do not receive, because you ask wrongly, to spend it on your passions." James 4:3

"Then you will call upon me and come and pray to me, and I will hear you. You will seek me and find me, when you seek me with all your heart." Jeremiah 29:12-13

"And without faith it is impossible to please him, for whoever would draw near to God must believe that he exists and that he rewards those who seek him." Hebrews 11:6

"'And whenever you stand praying, forgive, if you have anything against anyone, so that your Father also who is in heaven may forgive you your trespasses.'" Mark 11:25

11. Does this mean that our prayers will not be answered unless we are totally free from sin and personal weaknesses?

No. No one is totally free from sin or personal weaknesses. If we repent and ask for forgiveness, we will be restored to a right relationship with God. However, if we deliberately continue to sin without repentance or genuine sorrow for our sins, God will definitely be displeased with us and our prayers may not be answered.

Scripture References

"Whoever conceals his transgressions will not prosper, but he who confesses and forsakes them will obtain mercy." Proverbs 28:13

"When I kept silent, my bones wasted away through my groaning all day long.. .. I acknowledged my sin to you, and I did not cover my iniquity.. .. and you forgave the iniquity of my sin. Therefore let everyone who is godly offer prayer to you at a time when you may be found." Psalm 32:3-6

"Create in me a clean heart, O God, and renew a right spirit within me.. .. Then I will teach trans-gressors your ways, and sinners will return to you." Psalm 51:10,13

12. Are there any other reasons (besides those referred to above) why God might not grant us what we ask for?

Yes. God may not grant what we ask for if our desires or requests are not in accord with his own will or purposes.

Scripture References

"'As the heavens are higher than the earth, so are my ways higher than your ways and my thoughts than your thoughts.'"
Isaiah 55:9

To the Christians in Rome Paul wrote: *"(You are) always in my prayers, asking that somehow by God's will I may now at last succeed in coming to you. I have often intended to come to you (but thus far have been prevented), in order that I may reap some harvest among you as well as among the rest of the Gentiles."*
Romans 1:10, 13

Paul wrote: *"So to keep me from being too elated by the surpassing greatness of the revelations, a thorn was given me in the flesh, a messenger of Satan to harass me, to keep me from becoming too elated. Three times I pleaded with the Lord about this, that it should leave me. But he said to me, 'My grace is sufficient for you, for my power is made perfect in weakness.' Therefore I will boast all the more gladly of my weaknesses, so that the power of Christ may rest upon me. .. For when I am weak, then I am strong."* 2 Corinthians 12:7-10

Jesus himself prayed: *"'My Father, if it is possible, let this cup pass from me; nevertheless, not as I will, but as you will.'"*
Matthew 26:39

13. Is prayer primarily a matter of asking God for things we want or need?

No! Prayer does include requests or petitions, but it also involves praise, confession, and thanksgiving. If the only time we pray is when we want or need something from God for ourselves or others, we do not have the kind of fellowship with God which he wants us to have.

Scripture References: CONFESSION

"'O my God, I am ashamed and blush to lift my face to you, my

God, for our iniquities have risen higher than our heads, and our guilt has mounted up to the heavens." Ezra 9:6

"I [Daniel] turned my face to the Lord God, seeking him by prayer and pleas for mercy with fasting and sackcloth and ashes. .. we have sinned and done wrong and acted wickedly and rebelled, turning aside from your commandments and rules." Daniel 9:3-5

Scripture References: THANKSGIVING

"Do not be anxious about anything, but in everything by prayer and supplication with thanksgiving let your requests be made known to God." Philippians 4:6

"Pray without ceasing, give thanks in all circumstances; for this is the will of God in Christ Jesus for you." 1 Thessalonians 5:17-18

"Enter his gates with thanksgiving, and his courts with praise! Give thanks to him; bless his name!" Psalm 105:4

Scripture References: PRAISE

"Oh come, let us worship and bow down; let us kneel before the LORD, our Maker! For he is our God, and we are the people of his pasture, and the sheep of his hand." Psalm 95:6-7

"I will bless the LORD at all times; his praise shall continually be in my mouth." Psalm 34:1

14. Is it better to pray alone or to pray with others?

It's important for us to pray frequently when we are alone with God. However, it's also important for us to pray frequently with others. The Bible has many examples of both individual prayers and the prayers of larger groups of people who join their voices and hearts together in bringing their praise and petitions to the Lord.

Scripture References

"'When you pray, go into your room and shut the door and pray to your Father who is in secret. And your Father who sees in secret, will reward you.'" Matthew 6:6

"'I say to you, if two of you agree on earth about anything they

ask, it will be done for them by my Father in heaven. For where two or three are gathered in my name, there am I among them.'"
Matthew 18:19-20

"All these with one accord were devoting themselves to prayer."
Acts 1:14

"So Peter was kept in prison, but earnest prayer for him was made to God by the church.. .. many were gathered together and were praying." Acts 12:5,12

15. Is it desirable for us to fast when we pray?

Many people fasted in Bible times and many still do so today. Fasting is good if it helps us focus our hearts and minds on God and if it is a genuine sign of reverence, sincerity and humility before God. We should not fast, however, in order to try to earn favor with God. God may "reward" our prayer and fasting, but he grants us his blessing because of his own mercy and grace and not on the basis of our merits.

Scripture References
"'[Ezra] proclaimed a fast there, at the river Ahava, that we might humble ourselves before our God, to seek from him a safe journey for ourselves, our children, and all our goods.. .. So we fasted and implored our God for this, and he listened to our entreaty.'" Ezra 8:21-23

"'As soon as I [Nehemiah] heard these words I sat down and wept and mourned for days, and I continued fasting and praying before the God of heaven.'" Nehemiah 1:4

"'I [Daniel] turned my face to the LORD God, seeking him by prayer and pleas for mercy with fasting and sackcloth and ashes.'" Daniel 9:3

"She [Anna] did not depart from the temple, worshiping with fasting and prayer night and day." Luke 2:37

"They [Paul and Barnabas] had appointed elders for them in every church, with prayer and fasting they committed them to the Lord in whom they had believed." Acts 14:23

16. Does God give us only those things we ask for in prayer?

No. God often grants us far more than we ask, much more than we deserve, and at times even more than we can imagine. Besides, sometimes we are too sick, too tired, or too confused to know what to ask for.

Scripture References
"Now to him [God] who is able to do far more abundantly than all we ask or think, according to the power at work within us, to him be glory in the church and in Christ Jesus. .. forever and ever." Ephesians 3:20
God said to Solomon: *"'I now do according to your word.. .. I give you also what you have not asked.'" 1 Kings 3:12-13*
"'But seek first the kingdom of God and his righteousness, and all these things will be added to you.'" Matthew 6:33
"'Put me to the test,' says the LORD of hosts, 'if I will not open the windows of heaven for you and pour down for you a blessing until there is no more need.'" Malachi 3:10

17. What is meant by "The Lord's Prayer"?

That is the prayer which Jesus taught his disciples.

Scripture Reference
"'Our Father in heaven, hallowed be your name. Your kingdom come, your will be done, on earth as it is in heaven. Give us this day our daily bread, and forgive us our debts, as we also have forgiven our debtors. And lead us not into temptation, but deliver us from the evil one. Matthew 6:9-13

Exploring Further

1. What is prayer?

In its simplest form, prayer is communicating with God. That communication usually finds expression in spoken words or conscious thoughts. However, at times people also communicate with God through tears of confession, unspoken longings, unexpressed desires, or other ways of directing their hearts and minds to the Lord. In this lesson the focus is on communication with God through spoken words or unspoken thoughts.

2. **Does a person have to be a born again believer in order to pray to God? Does a person have to be born again in order to have his prayers answered?**

The answer to both questions is NO. God is very gracious and invites every sincere person to share his deepest feelings and longings with him in prayer. Not only is God willing to hear and listen to the prayers of those who sincerely and humbly seek him, he also often answers them. Students will probably be able to give examples of God's answers to the prayers of people who are not (yet) believers but who sincerely cry out to God—even when they are not sure that God exists. God does not promise to answer the prayers of everyone in the way they desire, but his ears are open to all who earnestly seek him and cry out to him.

Consider the following passages: Deuteronomy 4:20; 1 Kings 8:46-50; Isaiah 14:1-5; Isaiah 55:1, 6-7; Psalm 65:2; Psalm 78:34; Joel 2:13; Malachi 3:7-8; Luke 11:10; Luke 15:20.

3. **Is it desirable to have "set times" for prayer? Or is it better to pray only when we "feel like" praying, so that our prayers will be genuine and sincere?**

It's very helpful to have set times for prayer each day, since this will almost certainly strengthen our prayer life. If we don't have "set times," it is easy to neglect praying because of busyness, laziness, interruptions, tiredness or forgetfulness. Most of those who are known for their strong prayer life do have set times for prayer and usually also pray frequently throughout the day (or night) when they are aware of any special need or blessing—whether in their own life or in the lives of others.

An effective prayer life does not come "automatically" when we become Christians. Many people, even very sincere people, let their prayer life slip to the point where they are no longer intense and passionate about prayer and spend less and less time praying. And as they pray less often or less fervently, they lose their sweet communion with the Lord, they see fewer answers to their prayers, and they become less effective in their Christian life.

Jesus himself prayed frequently and fervently. Paul was also a man of prayer. And in the Old Testament, Daniel was known for his faithful prayers and the wonderful answers he received as a result of his faithfulness. See, for example, Luke 5:16; Luke 18:1; 1 Thessalonians 5:17-18; and Daniel 6:10.

4. How can we strengthen our prayer life?

Students may be able and willing to share some of the ways in which they were able to strengthen their own prayer lives. If they do not have specific suggestions in this regard, the following suggestions may be helpful. It is helpful to maintain some kind of schedule for regular, daily prayers. Included will be prayers in the morning after rising, prayers in the evening before retiring, and prayers at meal times. It is also helpful to develop and maintain a list of things for which to pray. This list should be readily accessible, if possible, so that you can write things down whenever you think of them—and before you forget them. It is also helpful to maintain a record of prayers that have been answered in a special way. Looking back over your list of answered prayers will give you additional incentive to pray about other significant things that come to your attention. Also, when you see on your prayer list things that have not (yet) been answered in some definite way, you will be reminded to pray again for them. It is also helpful to write down the date when you first prayed for a specific need or situation and, when appropriate, the time when the prayer was answered.

It can also be very beneficial to have some set times for praying with others. By doing so, you can encourage one another while also being made aware of other special needs and concerns for which to pray.

Some people are also blessed and encouraged to pray by reading stories or articles or books on prayer. It's a great blessing to read the stories of great prayer warriors in the past (or present) who are exceptionally faithful and effective in their prayer life. It can also be instructive and helpful at times to read the prayers which have been offered by others. Sometimes it may become somewhat "routine" to pray all the time for the same things in the same way. By reading (or hearing) the prayers of others, you may be able to add a certain richness and effectiveness and diversity to your own prayers.

5. **What are some reasons why God might not answer our prayers in the way we would like?**

The Lesson notes provide a number of reasons why God doesn't always answer our prayers in the way we would like. Included are such things as disobedience, secret or unconfessed sins, indifference, selfish, pride, a lack of concern for others, a desire to have things that are not good for us, our intention to use what God gives us for purposes that do not honor or please him, or praying for something which is contrary to the will of God.

We should not always conclude, however, that the reason some of our prayers are not answered in the way we desire is because of sin in our lives or because of wrong motives. At times God withholds things we desire because he knows what is best for us and he knows that his will for us is much better than anything we ourselves might desire or ask for.
Read some of the following passages to gain a clearer and fuller understanding regarding what we call "unanswered" prayers: Deuteronomy 1:45; 1 Samuel 14:37; 1 Samuel 28:6; Psalm 66:18; Proverbs 1:28, 21:13; Zechariah 7:13; James 1:6-7; James 4:3. See also Exodus 33:20; Deuteronomy 3:26; 2 Samuel 12:16; Ezekiel 20:3; 2 Corinthians 12:8.

6. **Is there any value in fasting along with our prayers?**

Yes! Appropriate fasting can help us pray more sincerely and enable us to focus more consistently on the things we are praying about. When we fast, we may be able to get our minds off earthly things, focus on God's mercy and grace, and take our praying more seriously. Fasting is not helpful, however, if it causes us to become less focused on our praying because of the weakness of our bodies or minds. Fasting is also inappropriate if we use it as a "bribe" of some kind or if we believe that we can merit something by our fasting. Fasting by itself does not merit anything! God's answers to our prayers are always by grace—whether we fast or whether we don't.

Fasting is relatively common in some Christian circles while almost totally absent in others. Both those who fast often and those who rarely or never fast should thoughtfully evaluate the reason why they do what they do. Perhaps students may have insight into all of this by evaluating their own tradition of fasting or not fasting. And those who presently do not fast might seriously ask why they do not do so and thoughtfully consider the possibility of doing so in the future.

7. What kinds of prayers seem to be offered most often: Prayers of Confession, Praise, Thanksgiving, or Request? How can we develop a good "balance" in our prayer life?

There may not be a definite answer to this question, but it seems that many people consider prayer to be primarily "asking for something." Though many people do add prayers of confession, praise and thanksgiving to both their private and public prayers, prayers of petition or request often seem to dominate. Perhaps this is somewhat understandable, but it is unfortunate if prayer is understood to be primarily a matter of placing our requests before God.

It is also important to make sure that our prayer "requests" do not focus primarily on material blessings for ourselves — especially if those requests go well beyond the things we really need. In the Lord's Prayer there definitely is a strong emphasis on "requests," but those requests include the opening "petitions" that

God's name be hallowed, that his kingdom come, and that his will be done. There is also a request for "daily" bread, but there is no request for lots of other material things. Another request is for forgiveness of sins and for the grace to be able to resist and overcome temptation. Finally there is the element of praise, as the prayer concludes with the words: "*Yours is the kingdom and the power and the glory forever.*" (Note: these last words are very familiar to many believers, but they are not found in many early copies of the Bible.)

Perhaps one of the best ways to make sure that we don't focus too much on material things is by deliberately and thoughtfully including specific elements of praise and thanksgiving in our prayers. It may even be helpful to write out some things about which we should be praying, so that we do not neglect them.

Students may have some significant suggestions of their own on how we can best maintain an appropriate "balance" in our prayers.

8. What are the benefits of praying alone? What are the benefits of praying with others?

Praying alone should help us focus our thoughts and desires on the fact that we are talking directly with God himself. When praying alone, we will most likely include some of our very personal needs, our struggle with certain sins, and our thankfulness for the special blessings we have personally received or enjoyed things we might not wish to verbalize when we are praying with others. And, while praying alone, we can pour out our hearts to the Lord without being concerned about the reactions of others to our tears, passion or exuberance.

Praying with others can also be very beneficial, since others may pray about important matters which we have forgotten or not thought of. Others may also help us to focus on God and the things of his kingdom at a time when pressing personal concerns make it difficult for us to do so. And we can profit from the spiritual gifts and talents of others who seem to have the special gift of praying in a way that many others cannot do. It's also often encouraging to be joined together with other members of the family of God as we bring our praise and thanksgiving to the One who is the source of all our blessings.

Again, students may be able to share some significant thoughts and ideas which will help each of us develop a more fruitful and meaningful prayer life.

9. Is it desirable for us to share with others God's answers to our prayers? Should we also share with others the times when God does not seem to answer our prayers?

The answer to both questions is YES. Others will often be encouraged when they hear how God has answered the prayers of fellow believers. It will not only lead them to give thanks to God for his answers to the prayers of others; it will also help them to anticipate God's answers to their own prayers. And it will also encourage them to continue presenting their thanks and praise, as well as their petitions, to the Lord in fervent prayer.

But if believers will be encouraged to pray by God's answers to the prayers of others, will they not be discouraged from praying if they hear about prayers that were not "answered"? Not necessarily. If people hear only about answered prayers, they might begin to wonder why some of their own prayers have not been answered. But if they hear that other people also have both answered and "unanswered" prayers, they may be encouraged to continue praying in faith and confidence—even if the Lord has good reasons not to answer some prayers in the way they desired.

10. Is the Lord's Prayer more important or more sacred than other prayers?

Not really. The Lord's Prayer is obviously of very great importance since it was taught by Jesus himself. However, some people think that this prayer was intended to be a "model" prayer for us to follow without necessarily limiting our words to the brief prayer which Jesus taught. Jesus himself spent many hours in prayer when he was by himself, so it is very unlikely that he wanted us to pray this prayer over and over again without adding many thoughts and petitions of our own. It's also important to remember that the entire Bible has been inspired by God so that no parts of the Bible are more "sacred" than others. Even so, it's highly desirable for all believers to learn and pray this prayer which is the only prayer that Jesus taught his disciples.

Lesson Nine: Marriage and Family

Introduction

One of the most important areas of Christian living is that of marriage and the family. Even those who do not marry do interact with parents, brothers and sisters or with other people who are married, so everyone can profit from learning what the Bible teaches about this subject. Marriage customs differ greatly from one place or time to another, but there are some fundamental truths which are relevant for people everywhere.

Read thoughtfully what the Bible says about the proper relationship between husbands and wives and between parents and their children.

1. Where did the idea of marriage come from?

From God himself. In the beginning God created a male and a female who would come together in a loving relationship and eventually produce children like themselves.

Scripture Reference
"So God created man in his own image, in the image of God he created him; male and female he created them. And God blessed them and said to them, 'Be fruitful and multiply and fill the earth and subdue it.'" Genesis 1:27-28
"'He who created them from the beginning made them male and female, and said, "Therefore a man shall leave his father and his mother and hold fast to his wife, and the two shall become one flesh'." So they are no longer two but one flesh. What therefore God has joined together let not man separate.'" Matthew 19:4-6

2. Should everyone seek to be married?

Not necessarily. The Bible highly commends marriage but

also recognizes that some persons choose not to marry for good and sincere reasons which are acceptable to God.

Scripture References
"He who finds a wife finds a good thing and obtains favor from the LORD." Proverbs 18:22

"An excellent wife who can find? She is far more precious than jewels. The heart of her husband trusts in her, and he will have no lack of gain." Proverbs 31:10-11

"The unmarried man is anxious about the things of the Lord, how to please the Lord. But the married man is anxious about worldly things, how to please his wife, and his interests are divided. And the unmarried woman or betrothed woman is anxious about the things of the Lord, how to be holy in body and spirit. But the married woman is anxious about worldly things, how to please her husband. I say this for your own benefit, not to lay any restraint upon you, but to promote good order and to secure your undivided devotion to the Lord." 1 Corinthians 7:32-35

3. What does the Bible teach about the husband's role in marriage?

The husband is the head of the home and should love his wife just as Christ loved the church, his spiritual bride, and sacrificed his life for her.

Scripture References
"For the husband is the head of the wife even as Christ is the head of the church.. .. Husbands, love your wives, as Christ loved the church and gave himself up for her.. .. In the same way husbands should love their wives as their own bodies. He who loves his wife loves himself." Ephesians 5:23,25,28

"Husbands, live with your wives in an understanding way, showing honor to the woman as the weaker vessel, since they are heirs with you of the grace of life, so that your prayers may not be hindered." 1 Peter 3:7

4. What does the Bible teach about the wife's role in marriage?

Wives should love their husbands and submit to them just as believers submit themselves to Christ, their spiritual husband. If husbands love their wives with wholehearted and sacrificial love—as Christ loved the church—it will not be difficult for wives to submit to their husbands since they will be confident that their husbands will always be seeking what is truly best for them.

Scripture References
"Wives, submit to your own husbands, as to the Lord." Ephesians 5:22
"Do not let your adorning be external...but let your adorning be the hidden person of the heart with the imperishable beauty of a gentle and quiet spirit...For this is how the holy women who hoped in God used to adorn themselves, by submitting to their husbands." 1 Peter 3:3-5

5. How is the relationship between a husband and wife like the relationship between God and his chosen people and the relationship between Christ and believers?

God referred to himself as the "husband" of the people of Israel. He loved them, blessed them, protected them, made a covenant with them, and gave them special promises. In the New Testament, the church is referred to as the bride of Christ. Christ loved the church, prayed for her, and gave his life for her. This special love and care is a wonderful example of the kind of love husbands should have for their wives.

Scripture References
"For your Maker is your husband. .. the Holy One of Israel is your Redeemer." Isaiah 54:5
"'I have loved you with an everlasting love; therefore I have continued my faithfulness to you.'...'I was their husband, declares the LORD.'" Jeremiah 31:3, 32
"The marriage of the Lamb [Jesus] has come, and his Bride has made herself ready." Revelation 19:7

"'Come, I will show you the Bride, the wife of the Lamb.'"
Revelation 21:9

6. What does the Bible teach about faithfulness to our marriage partners?

Marriage partners should be faithful to each other at all times and in every way.

Scripture References

"Let marriage be held in honor among all, and let the marriage bed be undefiled, for God will judge the sexually immoral and adulterous." Hebrews 13:4

"Guard yourselves in your spirit, and let none of you be faithless to the wife of your youth." Malachi 2:15

"Drink water from your own cistern, flowing water from your own well.. . Let them be for yourself alone, and not for strangers with you." Proverbs 5:15, 17

"Why should you be intoxicated...with a forbidden woman and embrace the bosom of an adulteress? For a man's ways are before the eyes of the Lord, and he ponders all his paths." Proverbs 5:20-21

7. What does the Bible teach about divorce?

God intended from the beginning that marriage should be permanent. In Old Testament times, however, Moses permitted some people to divorce their wives because of the "hardness of their hearts." In New Testament times, Jesus reminded people that God's *intention* from the beginning was that marriage was to be a life-long arrangement.

Scripture References

Jesus said: *"'Moses allowed you to divorce your wives, but from the beginning it was not so. And I say to you: whoever divorces his wife, except for sexual immorality, and marries another, commits adultery.'" Matthew 19:8-9*

"For a married woman is bound by law to her husband while he lives, but if her husband dies she is released from the law of marriage. Accordingly, she will be called an adulteress if she

lives with another man while her husband is alive. But if her husband dies, she is free from that law, and if she marries another man she is not an adulteress." Romans 7:2-3

8. What should a believer do if his or her partner is not a believer?

Believers should not seek a divorce if their unbelieving partners are willing to continue living with them. Believing wives should be submissive to their unbelieving husbands in all things lawful and appropriate and continue to live pure and holy lives.

Scripture References
"Wives, be subject to your own husbands, so that even if some do not obey the word, they may be won without a word by the conduct of their wives--when they see your respectful and pure conduct." Peter 3:1,2
"If any brother has a wife who is an unbeliever, and she consents to live with him, he should not divorce her. If any woman has a husband who is an unbeliever, and he is consents to live with her, she should not divorce him.. .. But if the unbelieving partner separates, let it be so. In such cases the brother or sister is not enslaved." 1 Corinthians 7:12-15

9. What does the Bible teach about having more than one marriage partner?

From the very beginning, God's intention for marriage was that men should have only one wife and women should have only one husband. Though there were plural marriages in certain Old Testament times, these marriages often led to jealousy or other problems. Jesus and the apostles made it clear that believers should have only one marriage partner and that they should be faithful to each other as long as they both lived.

Scripture References
"Therefore a man shall leave his father and mother and hold fast to his wife, and they shall become one flesh." Genesis 2:24
"He [the king] shall not acquire many wives for himself, lest his

heart turn away." Deuteronomy 17:17
"Each man should have his own wife and each woman her own husband." 1 Corinthians 7:2

10. What does the Bible teach about the physical (sexual) side of marriage?

Sexual relations within the bonds of marriage are good, desirable, and a gift of God. Both husbands and wives should be very sensitive to the needs and desires of their partners. They should not make unreasonable demands or take advantage of one another or do anything that would hurt their partner either physically or emotionally.

Scripture References
"Enjoy life with the wife, whom you love. .. that he [God] has given you." Ecclesiastes 9:9
"Because of the temptation to sexual immorality, each man should have his own wife and each woman her own husband." 1 Corinthians 7:2
"The husband should give to his wife her conjugal rights, and likewise the wife to her husband. For the wife does not have authority over her own body, but the husband does. Likewise the husband does not have authority over his own body, but the wife does. Do not deprive one another, except perhaps by agreement for a limited time, that you may devote yourselves to prayer; but then come together again, so that Satan may not tempt you because of your lack of self-control." 1 Corinthians 7:3-5

11. What does the Bible teach about same-sex marriage?

In both the Old and New Testaments, all homosexual relationships are condemned.

Scripture Reference
"If a man lies with a male as with a woman, both of them have committed an abomination; they shall surely be put to death; their blood is upon them." Leviticus 20:13
"Their women exchanged natural relations for those that are

contrary to nature; and the men likewise gave up natural relations with women and were consumed with passion for one another, men committing shameless acts with men and receiving in themselves the due penalty for their error." Romans 1:26-27 "Do not be deceived: neither the sexually immoral, nor idolaters, nor adulterers, nor men who practice homosexuality.. . will inherit the kingdom of God." 1 Corinthians 6:9-10

12. What does the Bible teach about having children?

The Bible regards the birth of children as a great blessing from the Lord.

Scripture References
"Behold, children are a heritage from the LORD, the fruit of the womb a reward. Like arrows in the hand of a warrior are the children of one's youth. Blessed is the man who fills his quiver with them!"Psalm 127:3-5
"Your wife will be like a fruitful vine within your house; your children will be like olive shoots around your table." Psalm 128:3
"He [God] gives the barren woman a home, making her the joyous mother of children." Psalm 113:9
"Isaac prayed to the LORD for his wife, because she was barren. And the LORD granted his prayer, and Rebekah his wife conceived." Genesis 25:21

13. What should parents do for their children?

Parents should teach their children, pray for them, discipline them in love, provide for them, and serve as good examples of how to live as a Christian.

Scripture References
"Train up a child in the way he should go; even when he is old he will not depart from it." Proverbs 22:6

"'These words that I command you today shall be on your heart. You shall teach them diligently to your children, and shall talk of

them when you sit in your house, and when you walk by the way, and when you lie down, and when you rise.'" Deuteronomy 6:6-7 David said to his son Solomon: *"'Be strong, and show yourself a man, and keep the charge of the LORD your God, walking in his ways, and keeping his statutes, his commandments. .. that you may prosper in all that you do and wherever you turn.'" 1 Kings 2:2-3*
"Fathers, do not provoke your children to anger, but bring them up in the discipline and instruction of the Lord." Ephesians 6:4
"The LORD reproves him whom he loves as a father the son in whom he delights." Proverbs 3:12

14. How should children respond to the teaching and discipline of their parents?

Children should obey their parents in all things lawful, accept their loving discipline, and follow their good example. When parents are old and unable to support themselves, children should help provide for them. When they do all these things, they will bring joy to their parents. When they don't, the result will be sorrow, loss, distress, and punishment.

Scripture References
"Children, obey your parents in the Lord, for this is right." Ephesians 6:1
"'Honor your father and your mother, as the LORD your God commanded you.'" Deuteronomy 5:16
"The father of the righteous will greatly rejoice; he who fathers a wise son will be glad in him." Proverbs 23:24
"A wise son makes a glad father, but a foolish son is a sorrow to his mother." Proverbs 10:1
"The one who keeps the law is a son with understanding, but a companion of gluttons shames his father." Proverbs 28:7

15. How do the deeds of parents affect the lives of their children?

The righteous deeds of parents often lead to the blessing of their children. The sinful deeds of parents often lead to problems, trials, and hurts in the lives of their children. The parents may establish a pattern of life that continues in the lives of their descendants and all of them are punished for the failures of their parents and grandparents as well as their own sins. Children do not always follow the good example of their parents, but when they do, they and their parents are both blessed by it.

Scripture References
"You show steadfast love to thousands, but you repay the guilt of fathers to their children after them." Jeremiah 32:18
"He [Ahaziah] did what was evil in the eyes of the LORD and walked in the way of his father and in the way of his mother." 1 Kings 22:52
"He [Jeroboam] walked in all the way of Asa his father. He did not turn aside from it, doing what was right in the sight of the LORD." 1 Kings 22:43

16. What is the most important decision believing parents can make regarding their children?

Parents should humbly and sincerely determine to serve as an example to their children by walking in the ways of the Lord, teaching their children to walk in the ways of the Lord, and serving the Lord with their entire family.

Scripture References
"'I have chosen him [Abraham], that he may command his children and his household after him to keep the way of the LORD by doing righteousness and justice, so that the LORD may bring to Abraham what he has promised him." Genesis 18:19
David said: *"'I will ponder the way that is blameless. .. I will walk with integrity of heart within my house." Psalm 101:2*
"He [Cornelius] was a devout man who feared God with all his household, gave alms generously to the people, and prayed continually to God." Acts 10:2
"'As for me [Joshua] and my house, we will serve the Lord.'" Joshua 24:15

Exploring Further

1. **Is it better for parents to choose marriage partners for their children or is it better for the marriage partners to make this decision themselves? If the Bible does not answer this question, how can we determine what is best?**

People will likely answer this question primarily on the basis of their own personal experience. For example, in places where parents traditionally choose marriage partners for their children, people will likely be inclined to find that this is definitely the better way. When people are brought up in an area where men and women choose their own marriage partners, they will likely think that this is the better way.

Does the Bible give us any clear teachings regarding this matter? Not specifically. In the early part of the Bible it seems that at least some parents played a very strong role in finding marriage partners for their children. Abraham, for example sent his servant to find a wife for his son Isaac (Genesis 24) and Isaac and his wife played a strong role in finding a wife for their son Jacob (Genesis 27:46 and Genesis 28 and 29). Judges 14:1-4 tells us something about the role of parents in the marriage of Samson. Other passages also indicate that parents "gave" a daughter to someone in marriage and the groom (or his parents) was expected to give an appropriate gift to the father for the "loss" of his daughter. (See Genesis 34:11-12; Genesis 29:18-20; 34:12; and Exodus 22:16-17.) In the New Testament Paul writes that older women should teach the younger women to love their husbands (Titus 2:4). This may indicate that the marriages he refers to were "arranged" marriages rather than "love" marriages. However, none of these passages contains a clear directive from God as to whether or not marriages should always be "arranged" by the parents. For the most part, both in Bible times and in history, marriages were arranged in different ways at different times and in different places. There would appear to be no specific arrangement which is the only one pleasing to God or the only one which is likely to produce a long and happy marriage.

It is usually very desirable, however, that Christian parents approve of a marriage. Parents have had many more life experiences than young people do and they are able to recognize potential problems or pitfalls which younger people may not see. It is also generally helpful for a bride and groom to have similar backgrounds, though this is not absolutely essential. It is very important, however, for the marriage partners to share a common faith. For Christians, this is not only important but also commanded. (See 1 Corinthians 7:39 and 2 Corinthians 6:14). It is also very helpful (if possible) for a bride and groom, before marriage, to have some meaningful counseling from people who are able to provide helpful guidance and direction. As most married people realize, it is not enough that a bride and groom have strong feelings for each other. Life has many dimensions and challenges, and potential husbands and wives should be made aware of these before they make a permanent commitment to love and live with each other as long as they both shall live. (See Paul's observations in 1 Corinthians 7:28 and 7:32-35).

2. **In Matthew 19:4-6 we read that "a man shall leave his father and his mother and hold fast to his wife." Does this mean that young couples should not live with their parents after they are married?**

Not necessarily. There are times and circumstances (such as a housing shortage or economic concerns) which make it necessary for young married couples to live with their parents. There may also be other situations where local customs expect young people to live with their parents for a while after they are married. However, Jesus' teachings in Matthew 19 would appear to indicate that a man and wife have stronger obligations to each other than to their parents. (See also Genesis 2:24 in this connection.) The newly married man should, as soon as possible, become the "head" of a new household and no longer occupy a secondary place in his home. The wife also should give her primary allegiance to her husband rather than to her parents. However, both husband and wife should seek to maintain a cordial and loving relationship with their parents, respecting them for who they are, and showing appropriate gratitude for all that they did for them during the years before their marriage.

3. **What are some reasons why it might be wise or desirable for a young man or woman to decide not to get married?**

There are various good reasons why a young person might choose not to marry. Consider what Paul writes about this in 1 Corinthians 7. Marriage can bring burdens and distractions as well as joys and blessings and the distractions might well interfere with a person's strong desire and commitment to serve the Lord in some special way. Paul himself chose to remain single for that very reason. Further, since there are many marriages that result in unhappiness or even divorce, a young person who is content to live a single life might understandably feel that he/she will live more happily without marriage. Others simply cannot find anyone they feel would make a suitable spouse. For them, it would not be worth the risk of living unhappily with someone for the rest of their life. There are also those who simply enjoy the freedom of living, working, traveling, and enjoying their hobbies and special interests without running the "risk" of marrying someone who would be a burden rather than a blessing. All of these reasons would seem to be legitimate if a person is able without too much difficulty to live a celibate life as Paul indicated in 1 Corinthians 7:8-9.

4. **One of the purposes of marriage is to produce children. Are there any good reasons why Christians should or may decide not to have children?**

In Bible times children were usually regarded as a precious gift from God. (See, for example, Genesis 30:19-20, Psalm 127:3-5 and 128:3-4.) Not being able to bear children was usually considered a great disgrace, a huge disappointment, and maybe even a punishment from God. (See Genesis 30:1-2, 22 and 1 Samuel 1:10-11.) Are there situations, then, when God is pleased with a couple's decision *not* to have children? Christians do not always agree on the "correct" answer to that question.

When married couples prayerfully seek to know God's will in this regard and then decide not to have children so that they can serve the Lord more effectively, most believers would seem to have no major problem with that decision. When couples choose not to have children because of the very difficult circumstances in which they live—such as very challenging economic problems, severe persecution of believers in their area, genuine health concerns or other pressing needs, many Christians would not challenge their decision. However, when couples choose not to have children simply so that they can spend more time and money on their own pleasures, some Christians would definitely question their decision. Ultimately, every decision that is made in regard to have children must be made prayerfully, humbly, and sincerely. Each of us must seek to serve the Lord to the very best of our ability without quickly judging the decisions of others.

5. **Husbands should love their wives as Christ loves the church and gave his life for the church. What should a Christian wife do if her husband does not love her or treat her with kindness, helpfulness and respect?**

Regrettably, the situation described here is very common. This may be especially true in areas where women have historically been treated as "second class citizens" or when a Christian woman has a non-Christian husband. However, it is also true in some Christian homes. The solution to this problem is not simple. In Christian homes, the husband should be patiently but strongly reminded what the Bible says about the divinely appointed roles of husbands in a marriage. Pastoral or other professional counseling may be both needed and helpful. Happily married couples could possibly meet with those in troubled marriages. Much prayer should be offered by those who know the situation and are concerned about it. Women who are familiar with broken situations should thoughtfully, lovingly, and prayerfully provide support for the wives whose husbands are unloving, unkind, or not very thoughtful. Wives with unloving husbands can also be given helpful literature to read on how faithful wives should deal with their domestic problems. In very many cases, however, the problem is never fully overcome. This is particularly true in cultures where women are generally treated poorly. In those cultures, husbands often do not consider their behavior to be inappropriate and they are not easily persuaded that it is. Students may have some helpful suggestions on this matter based on their own experience or on the experiences of others.

6. Should Christian wives obey their husbands if their husbands tell them to do something that is contrary to the teachings of the Bible?

Surprisingly, there are some who answer this question with a strong YES. They claim that husbands who tell their wives to do something wrong are responsible for the subsequent behavior of their wives, and the wives who faithfully do what their husbands tell them to do are themselves not guilty, no matter what they do. However, that is not true. Husbands do have some authority in the home, but they do not have a higher authority than God does. Wives (as well as the rest of us) must always obey God rather than man. (See Acts 4:19 and 5:29.)

7. Is divorce ever permissible for believers? Is re-marriage permissible for those who have been divorced on unbiblical grounds?

God hates divorce (Malachi 2:13-16), though in Old Testament times he permitted people to divorce their spouses on certain grounds because of the hardness of their hearts. (See Deuteronomy 24:1-4; Matthew 19:1-8.) In the New Testament, however, God makes it very clear that the only permissible ground for divorce is marital unfaithfulness on the part of one of the partners (Matthew 19:9). Most evangelicals understand "unfaithfulness" here to refer specifically to adultery. However, since the Greek word used here for "unfaithfulness" is not the same as the word for "adultery," some believe that "unfaithfulness" may possibly refer to other forms of unfaithfulness as well. From the very beginning, however, God intended that marriage would be permanent. .. and he still does!

If a person is divorced on grounds other than adultery of the spouse, that person should remain single or be reconciled to the spouse (1 Corinthians 7:11-12). However, if a person is divorced on the grounds of marital unfaithfulness, the spouse is free to marry and is not considered an adulterer (Matthew 19:9). (Note: In Leviticus 21:7 and 14 and in Ezekiel 44:22 we read that a priest was not permitted to marry either a widow or a divorced person—except for widows of priests. That prohibition is not repeated in the New Testament.)

8. **Homosexuality is becoming increasingly common in the world and even in the church. Should the church today accept a homosexual lifestyle as acceptable to God? If not, how should the church deal with homosexual persons who claim to be followers of Christ?**

Though homosexuality is becoming widely accepted in many societies, the Bible never condones a homosexual lifestyle for either men or women. The church, therefore, should not act as if homosexuality is now acceptable to God. It isn't. At the same time, we should recognize that for some people a homosexual lifestyle seems more "natural" than a heterosexual lifestyle. And, if people are convinced that something is "natural" rather than "chosen," they may feel that they are no longer responsible for their conduct. However, that does not make their conduct right or acceptable in the sight of God.

Those who are involved in a homosexual lifestyle should be treated with sincere and loving concern rather than simply being condemned for something which they feel is beyond their personal control. At times, professional help might also be recommended for those who would very much want to pursue a lifestyle that is pleasing to the Lord. At the same time they should be shown from the Bible (if they are willing to listen) that what seems "natural" is often sinful and wrong in the sight of God. They, like the rest of us, may often have to be reminded that what is right or wrong in God's sight is not determined by our natural feelings or tendencies but by what God himself teaches us in His Word.

9. **Some believers in the Old Testament (such as Abraham, Jacob, and David) had more than one wife and God did not seem to condemn them for that. Are there situations today where the church should regard polygamy as acceptable to God?**

Polygamy is generally not a major issue in most western cultures. However, it is still a major concern in some other cultures. Given the fact that Old Testament leaders often had more than one wife, it would seem fairly easy for believers in some cultures to justify their own polygamous practices. However, God created only one wife for Adam in the beginning and this seemed to be the divine pattern for marriage in the future. The pattern of having only one spouse is also the approved pattern for leaders in the New Testament. (See, for example, 1 Timothy 3:2 and 1 Timothy 3:12.)

A significant problem arises, however, when a man with several wives becomes a Christian and for the first time realizes what God's intention is for marriage. If the polygamist divorced all his wives but one, he would be "guilty" of divorcing innocent wives. In addition, the divorced wives might have an extremely difficult time providing for themselves and any children they might already have. They might also be looked down upon by others in the community and have very little opportunity to support themselves. In those situations, missionaries and other mature believers sometimes decide that the best thing they can do is to promote a monogamous lifestyle in the community and make sure than no new believers take more than one wife for themselves. They also appoint as leaders only those who have one spouse. At the same time, realizing that divorced wives would have an extremely difficult time in their culture, they permit polygamous men to continue to live with the wives they already have if they so choose. This may not be an ideal solution to the problem, but it does seek to meet the needs of people in "broken" situations in a loving and caring way.

10. What are some of the most important things that parents today can and should do for their children?

The answer to this question will depend at least partly on the situation where people are living. Students may therefore have various suggestions which will be particularly relevant for their own situation. However, there are some things which should be relevant in every culture or situation. Among them are the following: Parents should set an example for their children in every area of life. They should be people of integrity, perseverance, diligence, patience, love for family and others. They should also put Christ first in their lives, be faithful to their marriage partners and show them honor and respect, be faithful in worship, prayer, and study of the Scriptures.

They should seek to return good for evil, show kindness to those who may not treat them kindly, be sensitive to the needs of the poor, help those who are in need, and earnestly seek to stay away from anything and everything that would be displeasing to the Lord or hurtful to others. Sensitive parents will also spend quality time with their children, be sensitive to their needs and concerns, deal patiently with their weaknesses, encourage them as much as possible, discipline them in love, and pray faithfully for each child individually. They should also put much more emphasis on the treasures of heaven than on the accumulation of earthly goods. A good motto for all parents can be found in the Scriptures where Joshua boldly proclaimed: "As for me and my household, we will serve the Lord" (Joshua 24:1)

Lesson Ten: Suffering and Persecution

Introduction

The Bible tells us that in the life to come true believers will experience unending joy and perfect peace. In our present life, however, we often experience tears and trials, sickness and sadness, suffering and sorrow. Sometimes we suffer simply because we are human beings who live on a sin-cursed earth. At other times our suffering comes because we are faithful followers of Jesus Christ. Whatever happens to us, however, we have the confidence and assurance that Christ will never leave us or forsake us.

1. What does the Bible teach us about the suffering and trials which believers may experience?

Jesus told his followers that they would often face sufferings and trials if they faithfully sought to live for him and follow his example. Paul and other writers also emphasized that faithful believers would often suffer persecution because of their faith. Being a Christian in a hostile environment would not be easy. But persecution would also be an indication that the people being persecuted were faithful and true followers of Christ. And true followers of Jesus would never be forsaken by their Lord.

Scripture References

Jesus said: "'*In this world you will have tribulation. But take heart; I have overcome the world.*'" *John16:33*

Jesus said, "'*I chose you out of the world, therefore the world hates you.. .. A servant is not greater than his master. If they persecuted me, they will also persecute you.*'" *John 15:19-20*

Paul said: "*Through many tribulations we must enter the kingdom of God.*" *Acts 14:22*

Paul wrote: "*All who desire to live a godly life in Christ Jesus will be persecuted.*" *2 Timothy 3:12*

2. Are there any examples of persecution in the New Testament?

Yes, there are many. Church leaders and ordinary church members were often persecuted. Some were killed and many others were beaten or imprisoned. Paul suffered persecution in most of the places where he preached the Gospel, but he remained faithful. And, along with other believers, he continued to rejoice in the Lord and stayed strong in his faith in Jesus.

Scripture References
"There arose on that day a great persecution against the church in Jerusalem." Acts 8:1
"As servants of God we commend ourselves in every way: by great endurance; in afflictions, hardships, calamities, beatings, imprisonments, riots, labors, sleepless nights, hunger. .. as dying, and behold, we live; as punished, and yet not killed; as sorrowful, yet always rejoicing." 2 Corinthians 6:4, 5, 9, 10
"Do not be ashamed of the testimony about our Lord. .. but share in suffering for the gospel by the power of God." 2 Timothy 1:8-9
"To this you have been called, because Christ also suffered for you, leaving you an example, so that you might follow in his steps." 1 Peter 2:21

3. Doesn't God care that his children suffer persecution?

He certainly does. However, he promises that if we patiently endure suffering for Christ's sake, we will receive special blessings in this life and will receive a great reward in heaven when this life is over.

Scripture References
"Rejoice insofar as you share Christ's sufferings, that you may also rejoice and be glad when his glory is revealed." 1 Peter 4:13
Jesus said, *"'Blessed are you when others revile you and persecute you and utter all kinds of evil against you falsely on my account. Rejoice and be glad, for your reward is great in heaven.'" Matthew 5:11-12*
"We do not lose heart. Though our outer self is wasting away, our inner self is being renewed day by day. For this light momentary

affliction is preparing for us an eternal weight of glory beyond all comparison." 2 Corinthians 4:16-17

4. What are some of the ways in which persecution and trials can be a source of blessing in our present lives?

Trials and suffering for Christ's sake can help to strengthen our character, increase our joy, confirm our commitment to follow Jesus, increase our patience, prove the genuineness of our faith, teach us to depend on the Lord and not on our own resources, confirm our testimony and enable us to serve as an example to others. Persecution and trials may cause us sorrow, pain, and suffering, but they can also produce precious spiritual fruit in our lives.

Scripture References

"If you are insulted for the name of Christ, you are blessed, because the Spirit of glory and of God rests upon you." 1 Peter 4:14

"In this you rejoice, though now for a little while, if necessary, you have been grieved by various trials, so that the tested genuineness of your faith—more precious than gold. .. may be found to result in praise and glory and honor at the revelation of Jesus Christ." 1 Peter 1:6-7

"You became imitators of us and of the Lord, for you received the word in much affliction, with the joy of the Holy Spirit, so that you became an example to all the believers.. .. your faith in God has gone forth everywhere." 1 Thessalonians 1:6-8

"Count it all joy, my brothers, when you meet trials of various kinds, for you know that the testing of your faith produces steadfastness. And let steadfastness have its full effect, that you may be perfect and complete, lacking in nothing." James 1:2-4

"I want you to know, brothers, that what has happened to me has really served to advance the gospel.. .. And most of the brothers, having become confident in the Lord by my imprisonment, are much more bold to speak the word without fear." Philippians 1:12, 14

"We do not want you to be unaware, brothers, of the affliction we experienced. .. We were so utterly burdened beyond our strength

that we despaired of life itself. Indeed, we felt that we had received the sentence of death. But that was to make us rely not on ourselves but on God.. .. On him we have set our hope that he will deliver us again." 2 Corinthians 1:8-10

5. What encouragement does the Bible give to those who suffer persecution?

God will never leave or forsake those who suffer for Christ's sake. He will ultimately work out *all* things for the benefit of those who love him. And those who persevere to the end will inherit a crown of glory.

Scripture References
"God has said, 'I will never leave you nor forsake you.' So we confidently say, 'The Lord is my helper; I will not fear; what can man do to me?'" Hebrews 13:5-6
"Consider him [Jesus] who endured from sinners such hostility against himself, so that you may not grow weary or fainthearted." Hebrews 12:3
"Of this gospel I [Paul] was appointed a preacher and apostle and teacher, which is why I suffer as I do. But I am not ashamed, for I know whom I have believed, and I am convinced that he is able to guard until that Day what has been entrusted to me." 2 Timothy 1:11-12
"You had compassion on those in prison, and you joyfully accepted the plundering of your property, since you knew that you yourselves had a better possession and an abiding one." Hebrews 10:34
"If we endure, we will also reign with him." 2 Timothy 2:12
"And we know that for those who love God all things work together for good, for those who are called according to his purpose." Romans 8:28

6. What should we do if we suffer trials or persecution because of our faith?

We should commit our lives to the Lord, continue to live a Christian life, and concentrate on the glory to come. Though

172

present trials can be very severe, we should remember that they cannot begin to be compared with the glory that will someday be ours when we are with Christ.

Scripture References

"Let those who suffer according to God's will entrust their souls to a faithful Creator while doing good." 1 Peter 4:19

"We do not lose heart. Though out outer self is wasting away, our inner self is being renewed day by day. For this light momentary affliction is preparing for us an eternal weight of glory beyond all comparison, as we look not to the things that are seen but to the things that are unseen. For the things that are seen are transient, but the things that are unseen are eternal." 2 Corinthians 4:16-18

"I consider that the sufferings of this present time are not worth comparing with the glory that is to be revealed to us." Romans 8:18

7. What attitude should we have toward those who persecute us?

We should not seek "to get even" with them, but leave revenge to God, trusting that he will do what is just and right. As difficult as it may be, we should love them in Christ, pray for them and seek to do them good. Jesus himself is our example of how we should live among people who oppose us, oppress us, or persecute us. This is something we cannot do in our own strength, but something we can do through the indwelling power of Christ. It is his love that wins a victory—even if we have to die for our faith.

Scripture References

"Christ also suffered for you, leaving you an example, so that you might follow in his steps.. .. When he was reviled, he did not revile in return; when he suffered, he did not threaten, but continued entrusting himself to him who judges justly." 1 Peter 2:21, 23

"Beloved, never avenge yourselves, but leave it to the wrath of God, for it is written, 'Vengeance is mine, I will repay, says the Lord.' To the contrary, 'if your enemy is hungry, feed him; if he is thirsty, give him something to drink;".. . Do not be overcome by

evil, but overcome evil with good." Romans 12:19-21
Jesus said: *"'Love your enemies and pray for those who persecute you, so that you may be sons of your Father who is in heaven.'" Matthew 5:44-45*
"Do not repay evil for evil or reviling for reviling, but on the contrary, bless, for to this you were called that you may obtain a blessing." 1 Peter 3:9

8. Does God promise that He will always keep believers from illness or injury or will heal them miraculously if they are sick, injured, suffering or persecuted?

No. Sometimes believers are miraculously healed when they are sick or injured, and sometimes they are spared from injury or sickness or accident through the special grace of God. But not always. Both believers and unbelievers often suffer and die from the same diseases and afflictions. And both believers and unbelievers often suffer and die from accidents or in floods or hurricanes or other natural disasters. In addition, believers in many parts of the world also face persecution because of their faith. God does love and protect and care for his children in very special ways, but he does not promise that they will escape all the suffering and trials that others experience.

However, as believers we have the assurance that nothing can happen to us outside the will of God. We also have the promise and assurance that everything that takes place in our lives will ultimately, in some way, turn out for our good. So we pray in faith that God will keep us from injury or accident and sickness in the confidence that such prayers are often answered. But if we are not spared from these things or if we are not immediately healed, we have the confidence that God can use unpleasant or painful situations to help us become the kind of persons he wants us to be. And if our sickness or accident or injury ends in death, we know that we will be taken into the glorious presence of our Savior where we will forever be free from sickness, suffering or pain.

Scripture References

"It is good for me that I was afflicted, that I might learn your statutes.. .. I know, O LORD. .. that in faithfulness you have afflicted me." Psalm 119:71, 75

"For the moment all discipline seems painful rather than pleasant, but later it yields the peaceful fruit of righteousness to those who have been trained by it." Hebrews 12:11

"To keep me from becoming conceited. .. a thorn was given me in the flesh, a messenger of Satan, to harass me.. .. Three times I pleaded with the Lord about this, that it should leave me. But he said to me, 'My grace is sufficient for you, for my power is made perfect in weakness.' Therefore I will boast all the more gladly of my weaknesses, so that the power of Christ may rest upon me. For the sake of Christ, then, I am content with weaknesses, insults, hardships, persecutions, and calamities. For when I am weak, then I am strong." 2 Corinthians 12:7-10

Exploring Further

1. **Do you believe that 2 Timothy 3:12 is true for every believer?**

   In some parts of the world most Christians would immediately answer this question with a strong YES. In other parts of the world, many Christians would probably say NO. In their own lives they experience little or no obvious persecution and may even be "rewarded" in some ways because of their honesty, faithfulness to their spouses, friendliness, and hard work. In general, however, living openly and consistently for Christ will eventually arouse enmity or opposition of one kind or another. Christians may be mocked on occasion because they do not participate in certain activities or attend certain places of entertainment. They may also be ridiculed for their refusal to go along with "the crowd" in some of the group activities at school or at work. They may also be considered "Bible fanatics" if they talk to other people about the Bible or read the Bible during their lunch hour or free time.

They may be called derogatory names because of their clean language, refusal to drink alcoholic beverages or gamble. They may be considered "radicals" because they attend church faithfully, observe a special day of the week as a day that is "holy unto the Lord," give generously to their church or mission organizations, and participate in "marches" to promote pro-life activities or other Christian causes. Christians who never face any kind of obvious "persecution" or opposition may simply be living in a strong Christian environment. However, there may also be many situations where a Christian is not persecuted in any way because he or she is not pursuing a distinctively Christian lifestyle and therefore does not stand out in the crowd of unbelievers.

2. **Can you give any personal examples of being persecuted because you are a Christian?**

Obviously, the answers students give to this question will vary from one person to another. It should be interesting, however, to see how students understand what persecution is. It should also be interesting and helpful to learn how each person has handled whatever persecution he or she has experienced.

3. **Wouldn't it be much better for us (believers) if we never experienced any suffering or trials or persecution in our lives?**

It might indeed be "easier" for us in some ways, but it would not necessarily be "better." Persecution often strengthens our faith, helps us to examine our lives to see what is really most important in life, blesses us to know that others look upon us as sincere followers of Jesus, challenges others to examine their own lives, increases our boldness to witness, brings glory and praise to God, creates joy in our hearts, produces and causes us to trust in the Lord rather than in our own abilities for provision, protection, and the things we need for daily living. See, for example, Acts 4:29-32; Acts 5:41-42; Philippians 3:10; Romans 8:17; 1 Peter 5:10.

4. **Why would anyone think he is offering a service to God if he killed Christians? (See John 16:2.)**

   Many non-Christians believe that Christians are deceiving people, teaching false things about God, dishonoring God by teaching that Jesus is the eternal Son of God, and leading people into all kinds of heretical and false teaching that lead them away from God rather than to God. Remember that the apostle Paul himself felt that way at one time and therefore hounded and persecuted believers (Acts 7:55-8:1; Acts 9:1; and Acts 22:19-20). Even Jesus himself was crucified because the Jewish leaders accused him of blasphemy, a great sin against God, when he taught that he was the Son of God (Matthew 26:63-66). Today, non-Christians in some countries put Christians to death because they believe that Christians are insulting God and spreading false teachings concerning him. In their own minds and hearts they sincerely believe that they are pleasing and serving God when they kill Christians.

5. **Do you think that those who suffer persecution in this life for Christ's sake will receive greater glory and greater reward in heaven? If so, what do you think this "glory" or reward will be like?**

   The Bible does seem to teach that those who suffer persecution for Christ's sake will receive some kind of special "reward" in their future life. Read, for example, Matthew 5:11 and Luke 6:22-23. However, the Bible does not explain specifically what this glory or crown or reward will be like. All believers will share in the glory and joy of being with Jesus for eternity, and this joy and glory will be far greater than anything any of us have ever experienced on earth. It's difficult to explain, therefore, how one person might have greater joy or blessing than another. There may well be some persons in heaven who will have special authority of one kind or another, but there will be no jealousy, pride, or envy of any kind. It's sufficient for us to know that the Bible has promised that the "reward" will be there even if we cannot fully understand what it will be like. Our greatest joy will not be our personal "position" or honor but the blessing and privilege of spending eternity with Jesus in a world of perfect peace and delight. Read some of the following passages and see how students understand all these things. Revelation 14:13; Revelation 20:4, 22:12; Hebrews 10:34, 11:26; 2 John 8; 1 Corinthians 3:8; 2 Timothy 4:8.

6. **Believers often experience trials or suffering that are not directly related to persecution. Do you think these "trials and suffering" will result in spiritual growth? Will they possibly also result in greater rewards in heaven? If so, do you think the "reward" will depend on how we respond to our trials in this life?**

The Bible may not give a specific answer to the question about future rewards in heaven, but it does clearly indicate that earthly afflictions often result in spiritual growth. In general, anything we do or any suffering we endure in a way that honors Christ will bring praise to him and may possibly also result in some kind of special reward in heaven. However, our primary emphasis in all of this should not be on ourselves and our possible future rewards but on Christ who is the author and source of everything "good" in our lives. To him belong the glory and honor and praise both now and forever. Read some of the following passages: Psalm 116:10; Psalm 119:67, 71, 75; Job 5:17; Malachi 3:3; John 15:2; 2 Corinthians 4:16-17; Hebrews 12:5 and 11; 1 Peter 1:7; Revelation 7:14.

7. **Can you think of any specific examples in your own life or in the life of someone you know in which trials and persecution resulted in "spiritual blessings" already in this life?**

Students may be able to refer to a variety of "challenging" experiences which resulted in spiritual benefits either for the persons who were involved or for others who heard about them.

8. **How should we respond to persons who treat us unfairly simply because we are Christians?**

We should definitely not return evil for evil! Nor should we immediately try to find weaknesses or failures in another person's life and focus on those in order to take the pressure off ourselves. If it is possible for you to discuss your faith openly and calmly with someone who is treating you unfairly, prayerfully take advantage of that opportunity. Most often, however, that will probably not be possible. Depending on your situation and circumstances, it might be possible to discuss your situation with a person of authority who can help you find an amicable solution to your situation. If, so, prayerfully take advantage of that opportunity if you can do so without doing unnecessary harm to yourself or to others who may be involved.

Also, in the spirit of Christ, you should seek to return good for evil and pray for the person or persons involved. You may possibly be able to quietly do something helpful and positive for someone who is treating you poorly. (See Proverbs 20:22; 24:29; 25:21; Matthew 5:38-48; Luke 6:27, 35; Romans 12:17-21; 1 Thessalonians 5:15; 1 Peter 3:9, 17.) It's important to remember, however, that you, like Jesus himself, will not necessarily be well-received by others, no matter what you do. In that situation, simply commend the entire matter to the Lord and patiently and prayerfully wait for His leading and guidance.

9. **How is your prayer life affected when you pray for healing or freedom from trials and persecution but God does not heal you or keep you from being persecuted?**

This is a very challenging question and will probably evoke a variety of responses. In general, students should recognize that throughout history many believers who prayed sincerely were not healed and many Christians who prayed sincerely were not spared from persecution or death. Both the Bible itself and the history of the church demonstrate that. Believers should also recognize, however, that God promises that he will never leave or forsake his people (Hebrews 13:6-7; Psalm 118:5-7;

Deuteronomy 31:6,8) and he will bring to glory those who die either from sickness or from persecution or in any other way (Hebrews 11:13-16; Revelation 14:13).

His purposes are sometimes accomplished most powerfully by those who remain faithful even when they are not healed or delivered. And since the ultimate goal in our lives is that God may be glorified through us, we should continue to trust in the Lord while also continuing to pray. See Hebrews 11:13-17 and 32-40 which record many victories while also referring to many people who suffered greatly but did not receive a victory in this present life. See also Hebrews 10:36. Also, remember that Jesus himself prayed very earnestly for a way to avoid his death on the cross, but God conquered sin through Jesus' death rather than sparing him from death (Matthew 26:39 and 42; Hebrews 2:10). God's ultimate purposes will surely be accomplished, though faithful followers of Jesus may have to suffer much from sickness, trials, poverty, or persecution. But through it all God will be glorified and in one way or another all those who trust in him will also ultimately share in his glory (Hebrews 13:13-14).

10. **In what way(s) would you be different if you were never sick or injured or in pain? Do you think you would be more fruitful, more joyful, and a better "witness" if everything in life went the way you wanted? Give the reasons for your answer.**
This is a question which must be answered individually by each student. Answers will likely vary significantly, but each student will likely have something worthwhile and helpful to share with others.

Lesson Eleven: The Future

Introduction

In this present life, believers often experience persecution, difficulties, suffering, and trials of various kinds. God never promised that it would be any different as long as we are on this earth. However, in the future it will be totally different! God has promised all true believers a glorious future of perfect joy and peace that will never end. This does not mean that our present trials are insignificant, but our knowledge of our wonderful future helps us during our times of trial to be patient and courageous as we look forward to the time when we shall be with the Lord forever.

1. What happens to us when we die as believers in Jesus.

Our earthly bodies die, but our spirits or souls are taken immediately into the presence of Jesus. The Bible does not tell us in detail what life is like for believers who die in the Lord, but it does give us the assurance that it is far better to be with the Lord than to continue living on this earth. Some believers teach that those who die as Christians will simply be "asleep" until the day of resurrection. According to those who hold this position, the departed "souls" of believers will be free from sorrow, pain and suffering, but they will not immediately experience the positive joy of being with the Lord. Most believers, however, teach that being with the Lord after they die is a time of glory and joy and blessing. They may have a different understanding of exactly what this involves, but they all are confident that being with the Lord is a greater blessing than anything they have ever experienced here on earth.

Scripture References

"We know that if the tent, which is our earthly home, is destroyed, we have a building from God, a house not made with hands, eternal in the heavens.. .. So we are always of good courage. We know that while we are at home in the body we are

away from the Lord." 2 Corinthians 5:1,6, 8

Paul wrote: *"For to me to live is Christ and to die is gain.. .. My desire is to depart and be with Christ, for that is far better." Philippians 1:21, 23*

"'Blessed are the dead who die in the Lord from now on.. . .that they may rest from their labors, for their deeds follow them!'" Revelation 14:13

2. What happens to our bodies when we die?

Our bodies eventually decay and return to "dust." They will not become alive again until Christ returns and all those who have died are resurrected. Though it is possible to "preserve" a body in some form so that it does not decay, bodies that have died will never return to their former state or condition. Death brings the end to a person's existence on earth. (It is true that a very small number of individuals have been revived after being declared dead, and a few have been raised back to life through the miraculous power of God, but these people all die "again" at some point.)

Scripture References

"'By the sweat of your face you shall eat bread, until you return to the ground, for out of it you were taken; for you are dust and to dust you shall return.'" Genesis 3:19

"Man is going to his eternal home. .. and the dust returns to the earth as it was,, and the spirit returns to God who gave it." Ecclesiastes 12:5, 7

3. When Christ returns to earth what will happen to our bodies?

Everyone who died will be raised to life again. Some will rise to an eternal life of glory while others will rise to shame and everlasting punishment.

Scripture References

"There will be a resurrection of both the just and the unjust." Acts 24:15

"'All who are in the tombs will hear his voice and come out,

those who have done good to the resurrection of life, and those who have done evil to the resurrection of judgment.'" John 5:28-29
"Many of those who sleep in the dust of the earth shall awake, some to everlasting life, and some to shame and everlasting contempt." Daniel 12:2

4. What will the resurrected bodies of believers be like?

The resurrected bodies of believers will be like the glorious "spiritual" body of Jesus Christ. They will have physical dimensions, just as the body of Jesus does, but they will be far more glorious than their earthly bodies ever were. They will be immortal and imperishable and will never be subject to any of the diseases, weaknesses or problems that our present bodies often have.

Scripture References
"The Lord Jesus Christ. .. will transform our lowly body to be like his glorious body." Philippians 3:20-21
"What is sown [buried] is perishable; what is raised is imperishable. It is sown in dishonor; it is raised in glory. It is sown in weakness; it is raised in power. It is sown a natural body, it is raised a spiritual body." 1 Corinthians 15:42-44

5. When will this all take place?

The resurrection of believers will take place when Jesus comes to earth again. We do not know when Jesus will return, but we look forward with great anticipation to this awesome time when Christ will be glorified and all who have longed for his appearing will rejoice.

Scripture References
Jesus said: *"'For this is the will of my Father, that everyone who looks on the Son and believes in him should have eternal life, and I will raise him up on the last day.'" John 6:40*
"Waiting for our blessed hope, the appearing of the glory of our great God and Savior Jesus Christ." Titus 2:13

"The Lord himself will descend from heaven with a cry of command, with the voice of an archangel and with the sound of the trumpet of God. And the dead in Christ will rise first." 1 Thessalonians 4:16

6. Who will see Jesus when he comes back to earth again?

Everyone! Though only a few people saw Jesus when he first came to earth as a baby in Bethlehem, every person who has ever lived will see him when he returns.

Scripture References
"'As lightning comes from the east and shines as far as the west, so will be the coming of the Son of Man.'" Matthew 24:27
"'Then will appear in heaven the sign of the Son of Man, and then all the tribes of the earth. .. will see the Son of Man coming on the clouds of heaven with power and great glory.'" Matthew 24:30
"Behold, he is coming with the clouds, and every eye will see him." Revelation 1:7

7. What will happen to the present universe when Jesus returns?

The universe as we know it will be destroyed and will be replaced by a new heaven and a new earth (Revelation 21:1). The "heaven and earth" referred to here refers to the heaven and earth that God created at the beginning of human history (Genesis 1:1). We do not know how the present universe will be destroyed, nor do we know whether this destruction will take place in a moment of time or through a longer process of some kind. However, we do know that the destruction will be universal and extremely dramatic. The "agent" of destruction will be "fire" just as the earlier destruction of the world at the time of Noah took place through water.

Scripture References
"The creation itself will be set free from its bondage to decay and obtain the freedom of the glory of the children of God." Romans 8:21

184

"The heavens will pass away with a roar. ... and the earth and the works that are done on it will be exposed.. . .the heavens will be set on fire and dissolved, and the heavenly bodies will melt as they burn! But according to his promise we are waiting for new heavens and a new earth in which righteousness dwells." 2 Peter 3:10-13 (See also 2 Peter 3:5-7)

"Then I saw a new heaven and a new earth, for the first heaven and the first earth had passed away." Revelation 21:1

8. When will Jesus return?

No one knows the exact time when Jesus will return. In his human nature even Jesus himself said that he did not know the day or hour when he would come back. However, there have been a number of people over the years who have predicted a specific time when Jesus would return. These predictions have led many people astray and have caused them to give away or sell their possessions or do other unusual things as they "prepared" for Christ's return. Those who make false predictions not only lead believers astray, but they also cause many unbelievers to scoff at the idea that Jesus will return some day.

Scripture References (Quotations from Jesus)
"'But concerning that day and hour no one knows. ... but the Father only.'" Matthew 24:36
"'Therefore, stay awake, for you do not know on what day your Lord is coming.'" Matthew 24:42
"'You also must be ready, for the Son of Man is coming at an hour you do not expect.'" Luke 12:40

9. Will believers be completely surprised when Jesus returns?

No. Though we don't know the exact time when Jesus will return, the Bible gives us various signs that will point to his coming. Those who read and believe what the Bible says will therefore be looking for and expecting Jesus' return and will not be surprised when he comes. Among the signs that point to Jesus' return are some that seem fairly common—such as wars, famines, natural disasters, persecution of believers, false teachings and an increase in disobedience and lawlessness.

There also are signs which will take place in the political and economic world. Some believers focus primarily on special events that will take place in the land of Israel and among the Jewish people before Jesus returns. Jesus himself pointed to one major sign that must be fulfilled before he returns and that is the preaching of the Gospel to the entire world. It is very interesting in this regard that the Gospel is reaching more people today than ever before in human history. In the light of all the things that have happened recently or are happening in the world today, many Christians believe that the return of Christ could well happen in our lifetime. However, whether Jesus returns soon or in the distant future, we should make sure that we are truly ready for his return!

Scripture References

"For you yourselves are fully aware that the day of the Lord will come like a thief in the night.. .. But you are not in darkness, brothers, for that day to surprise you like a thief." 1 Thessalonians 5:2, 4

Jesus said, *"'Many will come in my name, saying, "I am the Christ," and they will lead many astray. And you will hear of wars and rumors of wars.. .. Nation will rise against nation. .. and there will famines and earthquakes in various places.. .. Then they will deliver you up to tribulation and put you to death, and you will be hated by all nations for my name's sake. And then many will fall away and betray one another and hate one another. And many false prophets will arise and lead many astray. And. .. the love of many will grow cold. But the one who endures to the end will be saved.. .. And this gospel of the kingdom will be proclaimed throughout the whole world as a testimony to all nations, and then the end will come.'" Matthew 24:5-14*

"'When you see all these things, you know that he [Jesus] is near, at the very gates.'" Matthew 24:33

10. How should we believers live as we wait for Jesus to return?

We should live holy lives, encourage one another, share the Gospel with others, and look forward to the day of Christ's coming.

Scripture References
"So then let us not sleep, as others do, but let us keep awake and be sober. ... having put on the breastplate of faith and love, and for a helmet the hope of salvation. ... Therefore encourage one another and build one another up, just as you are doing." 1 Thessalonians 5:6-11

"What sort of people ought you to be in lives of holiness and godliness, waiting for and hastening the coming of the day of God. .. But according to his promise we are waiting for new heavens and a new earth in which righteousness dwells.. . .Therefore. .. be diligent to be found by him without spot or blemish, and at peace." 2 Peter 3:11-14

"The Lord is not slow to fulfill his promise, but is patient toward you, not wishing that any should perish, but that all should reach repentance." 2 Peter 3:9

11. What will happen to believers who are still living when Christ returns?

They will instantly be changed and will receive glorious and imperishable new bodies. They will then rise along with resurrected believers to meet Christ in the air and will live with him forever in glory.

Scripture References
"Behold! I tell you a mystery. We shall not all sleep [die], but we shall all be changed, in a moment, in the twinkling of an eye, at the last trumpet. For the trumpet will sound, and the dead will be raised imperishable, and we shall be changed." 1 Corinthians 15:51-52

"For the Lord himself will descend from heaven with a cry of command, with the voice of an archangel, and with the sound of the trumpet of God. And the dead in Christ will rise first. Then

we who are alive, who are left, will be caught up together with them in the clouds to meet the Lord in the air, and so we will always be with the Lord." 1 Thessalonians 4:16-17

12. What will Jesus do when he returns to earth?

He will raise to life all those who have died and will then judge everyone who has ever lived. This judgment is not to determine whether or not a person is saved, but will be a judgment of how people lived while on earth. Salvation is always by grace, but the lives people lived will reveal whether or not they were truly born again. God will graciously reward people for every good work they have done—even though he himself is the one who made it possible for them to perform these works. (See Ephesians 2:10.)

Scripture References
"'The Father... has given all judgment to the Son.'" John 5:22
"'Behold, the Lord came with ten thousands of his holy ones, to execute judgment.'" Jude 14-15
"'The Son of Man is going to come with his angels in the glory of his Father, and then he will repay each person according to what he has done.'" Matthew 16:27
"For we must all appear before the judgment seat of Christ, so that each one may receive what is due him for the things done in the body, whether good or evil." 2 Corinthians 5:10

13. What will happen to those who loved and served Jesus in this life?

They will receive the rewards which Jesus grants to those who loved and served him. They will also be welcomed into God's kingdom of glory where they will spend eternity with Jesus and all other believers in perfect love, joy, and peace.

Scripture References
Jesus said: *"'And if I go and prepare a place for you, I will come again and will take you to myself, that where I am you may be also.'" John 14:3*

"And when the Chief Shepherd [Jesus] appears, you will receive the unfading crown of glory." 1 Peter 5:4
"'Then the righteous will shine like the sun in the kingdom of their Father.'" Matthew 13:43

14. What will happen to those who did not believe and trust in Jesus?

They will also receive bodies of some kind though their bodies will be totally different from the spiritual, perfect bodies of believers. These bodies will be subject to suffering and pain without relief. They will be cast into the "fires of hell" away from the presence of God and his people. They will continue to exist under the judgment of God and will be eternally lost.

Scripture References
"'These [unbelievers] will go away into eternal punishment.'" Matthew 25:46
"They will suffer the punishment of eternal destruction, away from the presence of the Lord and from the glory of his might." 2 Thessalonians 1:9
"'The Son of Man will send his angels, and they will gather out of his kingdom all causes of sin and all law breakers, and throw them into the fiery furnace. In that place there will be weeping and gnashing of teeth.'" Matthew 13:41-42

15. What will life be like in the new heaven and earth for believers?

Life will be glorious beyond anything we can now imagine or describe. However, the Bible itself does not give us many specific details concerning this new life because we could not fully understand them. Rather, the Bible emphasizes the absence of things which often make our present lives difficult, challenging, frustrating or sorrowful. For example, in the life to come there will be no suffering, no sadness, no sickness, no death and no tears. There will be no darkness, no failures, no weaknesses, no disappointments and no unmet needs. The curse pronounced over the earth during the days of Adam will no longer exist. Life will be perfect in every way. Nothing in our present life can even begin to compare with what our future life will be like. We will live in joy and peace and glory with JESUS in a life that will never end.

Scripture References

"No eye has seen, nor ear heard, nor the heart of man imagined, what God has prepared for those who love him." 1 Corinthians 2:9

"'They will be his people, and God himself will be with them as their God. He will wipe away every tear from their eyes, and death shall be no more, neither shall there be mourning, nor crying, nor pain anymore, for the former things have passed away.'" Revelation 21:3-4

"No longer will there be anything accursed, but the throne of God and of the Lamb will be in it, and his servants will worship him. They will see his face, and his name will be on their foreheads. And night will be no more. They will need no light of lamp or sun, for the Lord God will be their light, and they will reign forever and ever." Revelation 22:3-5

Exploring Further

1. Do you look forward to the Second Coming of Jesus?

This question will likely evoke an interesting variety of responses from students. Student answers may depend on such things as the following: their current life circumstances, whether or not they have loved ones or friends who are not yet believers, their desire to serve the Lord for a much longer time with the talents and training and abilities they have, their understanding of some teachings in the Bible, or other personal interests or concerns.

2. Will believers get a glorious new body immediately after they die? If so, will this body be different from the body believers will receive at the time of the resurrection?

Many believers seem to have the impression that a Christian who dies will immediately receive a glorious new body like Christ's resurrection body. The Bible, however, does not teach that. Believers will not receive the body described in 1 Corinthians 15:35-49 or Philippians 3:20-21 until Christ returns and the dead in Christ shall arise. Until that time, believers exist in the presence of Christ in glory, but the Bible does not tell us what kind of "body" believers will have during the time between death and final resurrection. 2 Corinthians 5:1 may refer to that body, but this passage also may refer to the glorious body we shall ultimately have forever.

The book of Revelation does refer to believers during the time between their death and the time of resurrection, but much of the language in this book is figurative rather than literal. (See, for example, the "picture" of Christ presented in Revelation 1:12-17.) We also read in Revelation 6:9-11 about the souls of martyrs who had been killed for Christ's sake. These souls, described as being "under the altar," were given "white robes" to wear. (There is no reference in this passage to any kind of "bodies" which believers have at that point.) For those of us who live on earth in our physical bodies, it is difficult to understand how "souls" can be seen or how they can wear robes. Most readers, therefore, understand this language to be figurative rather than literal. Though it is difficult (or impossible) for us to say with certainty just what kind of "bodies" believers have during the interim period between death and resurrection, the Bible does clearly teach that believers will not receive their immortal, glorious, spiritual bodies until the time of the final resurrection.

3. Will everyone receive a "new body" of some kind at the time of the resurrection?

Yes. Since everyone will arise from the dead at the time of Christ's return, everyone will receive a new post-resurrection body. The new bodies of believers will be glorious, immortal, and spiritual (Philippians 3:20-21 and 1 Corinthians 15:35-54). The new bodies of unbelievers will be subject to suffering and pain and will in no way be glorious (Matthew 25:41, 46 and Mark 9:42-48). However, since the Bible does not describe the post-resurrection bodies of unbelievers in any detail, it would seem best not to speculate too much on what these bodies will be like. There is much we will not fully understand until the time when Christ returns.

4. What do you think it means that believers will receive a "spiritual" body when Jesus returns?

When Jesus arose from the grave, it clearly was the "natural, physical body" of Jesus which arose. Before his resurrection, the body of Jesus was lying lifeless and immobile in the tomb. After he arose, Jesus' body was no longer there. In some miraculous way the body of Jesus had been transformed by the power of God into a glorious new body. It was still physical in the sense that it could be seen and identified as the body of Jesus, but there were some wonderful new dimensions to that body. It was not "restricted" or "limited" in the way our present bodies are. Jesus could appear and then disappear at will.

He was no longer subject to tiredness, hunger, thirst, disease, suffering or death. He was still able to enjoy some of the things which we presently enjoy because we are physical beings, but he was essentially a "spiritual" being who was not limited, not mortal, and in no way affected by sin or by any of the results of sin. So, though in some ways it was a "physical body," it was also much more than that. And so it will be with our own "spiritual" bodies after our resurrection. Those bodies will still have physical characteristics of some kind, but they will be much more than what we know as "physical" today. They will never suffer from sickness or disease or weakness or death, and they will be far more wonderful than anything we have ever known on earth.

5. **Are we able to determine exactly when Jesus will return? Are we able to determine the approximate time when Jesus will return?**

Already in New Testament times, there were people who were very confident that Jesus would return in their lifetime. (See, for example, 2 Thessalonians 2:1-4.) One of the reasons for that is that many believers are very eager to have Christ return. Another reason is that some of the "signs" given in the Bible concerning the return of Christ can be interpreted in such a way that, in any age, they "prove" that Christ will return very soon. However, it is very unwise to make a prediction, as many have done, that Christ will come at a specific time. We simply do not know exactly when Jesus will return.

At the same time, the Bible does give us a number of "signs" that will precede the coming of Christ so that we may look expectantly for his return. Some of those signs are an increase in wars, rumors of wars, natural disasters, persecutions, false teachings, and wickedness (Matthew 24:4-12). There is also a phenomenal increase in "knowledge" and information. (Some believers see this as a fulfillment of Daniel 12:4.) These signs are certainly all present today, but they have also been present in one place or another in almost every other generation as well. Some believers therefore focus on what they consider to be a unique sign--the establishment of Israel in 1948 as an independent nation and the significant role that the tiny nation of Israel continues to play in our contemporary world.

Matthew 24:14 points to one additional sign which is truly very special. Here we read: "And this gospel of the kingdom will be preached in the whole world as a testimony to all nations, and then the end will come." Today the Gospel is reaching the world in a way that has never happened before. With modern technology, information can be spread much more quickly and much more widely. Many believers are using this new technology to translate the Bible, distribute the Bible, and make the Gospel message available through technology, the internet, radio, TV, audio Scriptures, social meda, and in various other creative ways.

We cannot say exactly when Christ will return, but at the very least believers should be alert, expectant, diligent, and eager to share the Gospel of Jesus with those people who have not yet heard it. Among the many passages that are relevant here are the following: Daniel 12:1-4; Matthew 24:3-44; Mark 13:3-37; Luke21:5-36; 1 Thessalonians 5:1-4; 2 Thessalonians 2:1-12; 2 Peter 3:8-12; Revelation 16:15, and 22:20.

6. How should we as Christians live as we wait for Jesus to return to earth?

We should be humble, wise, holy, faithful, loving and thoughtful. We should also eagerly be looking forward to the return of Christ while making the best possible use of our time, energy, resources, and all that the Lord has entrusted to us. We should stay away from anything and everything that would dishonor Christ, lead others astray, or cause us to put our roots too deeply into the things of this world while neglecting the things of the Kingdom of our Lord. Students will likely be able to suggest many things which are relevant for their own lives. Sincere believers may possibly disagree on certain specifics, but all of us should continue to live faithfully, wisely and expectantly as we eagerly look forward to the coming of Jesus. Read the following Scripture passages: 2 Peter 3:10-18; Philippians 1:9-11; Titus 2:11-14.

7. Christians have different views of the "millennium" (the thousand year reign of Christ described in Revelation 20). What are some of those differences? How important are those differences? What is your own view of the millennium?

There are basically three different views of the millennium called a-millennialism, pre-millennialism, and post-millennialism.

- **A-millennialism** teaches that the "thousand years" are not to be taken literally any more than some other things in the book of Revelation are. For example, Satan is referred to in Revelation 20:1-5 as a dragon and a serpent that is bound with a chain even though he is a spirit being which cannot be bound with material things. He is thrown into a pit, though spirit beings are normally not "thrown." He is put in a pit without a bottom, and the pit is locked and sealed. All of these things, as well as the "thousand years," are considered to be symbolic and are therefore not taken literally. According to the a-millennial interpretation, Satan is bound or limited after Christ's resurrection and ascension so that he is now limited in what he is able to do. The Good News of the Gospel will be preached in the whole world and Satan will not be able to prevent it. There will come a brief time, however, when Satan will again have great power and will strongly oppose the church, but as Jesus taught in Matthew 16:18, the powers of evil will not be able to prevail against it.

- **Pre-millennialism** teaches that the thousand year period, as well as the binding of Satan in a bottomless pit and the other things mentioned in Revelation 20:1-5, are to be understood literally. Jesus will return to earth before ("pre") the thousand years referred to. The millennium will be a period of great peace throughout the world, a time when righteousness will rule over the entire earth with Jesus himself serving as king over the world from his throne in Jerusalem. At the end of the thousand years, Satan will be released from the pit and will again have the power to deceive multitudes of people who will band together to oppose Jesus and his people. However, Satan will be defeated and destroyed. Jesus will then reign forever with his people in glory while Satan and his followers will exist forever in the place of punishment prepared for them. There are various versions of the pre-millennial position, but the explanation presented here is a basic component of each of them.

- **Post-millennialism** teaches that before Jesus returns to earth the church will grow tremendously throughout the world and Satan will not be able to stop it. In fact, the growth of the church will be so great that the teachings of Jesus and his kingdom will in some measure dominate most of the world. This period of phenomenal growth is referred to figuratively as the "millennium." Jesus will return to earth after ("post") the millennium. When he returns, all people who have died will be resurrected. There will then be a final judgment of all the people who have ever lived, resulting in eternal glory for the saved and eternal loss for those who are not.

The differences among these positions are definitely significant, but almost all Christians are in agreement that Jesus will return to the earth, all those who have died will be resurrected, all those who ever lived will be judged, Christ and his people will live forever in indescribable glory, and those who are not saved will be banished forever from the joy and glory of the saved. If students choose to discuss these differences at greater length, it is important that they not emphasize the differences so strongly that they fail to recognize and remember the things on which they agree!

8. How do you understand the "final judgment" the Bible refers to? Will people not know until the "final judgment" whether or not they are saved?

The Bible refers to a future judgment in various passages such as Matthew 24:50-51, 25:31-46; John 5:28-29; Revelation 20:11-15; Romans 2:1-11. See also 2 Corinthians 5:10; Matthew 11:20-22; Acts 17:31; 1 Corinthians 3:10-15; 2 Peter 2:9, 3:7; 1 John 4:17; and Jude 15. The judgment referred to in these passages is a judgment of our works. John 5:24 clearly teaches that if we truly believe in Jesus we have eternal life and will not be condemned. A few verses later, however, we read in John 5:28-29 that those who have done evil in their lives will be condemned. This passage teaches that a person's life will reveal whether or not he is truly a child of God. Those who persistently do evil demonstrate that they were never truly born again. At the same time we should also recognize that a person can be truly saved and still live in a way that is not productive for the kingdom of God (1 Corinthians 3:10-15). These people will not be lost, but on the Day of Judgment they will discover that nothing they have done in their lives is worthy of any kind of "reward" from the Lord (1 Corinthians 3:15).

When we sincerely repent of our sins and put our trust in Jesus to save us, we can know with certainty that we have eternal life. We do not have to wait until the judgment day to find out whether or not we are saved. However, we will have to wait until the Day of Judgment to learn how God has judged the way we have lived. In some situations, people who thought they were saved were never truly born again. In God's sight their actions revealed the absence of true saving faith in their lives and they will suffer an eternal loss (Matthew 25:41-46).

9. Will unbelievers have a "second chance" to believe in Jesus after He returns?

Hebrews 9:27 would appear to indicate that the answer to that question is definitely NO. This passage reads: *"Just as it is appointed for man to die once, and after that comes judgment.. ."* This interpretation would seem to be confirmed by Matthew 25:41-46 and 2 Corinthians 5:10. However, some of those who teach a pre-millennial interpretation of Revelation 20 suggest that non-believers who are living on earth at the time of Christ's return will have a "second opportunity" to commit their lives to Christ during the millennial period. But neither Revelation 20 nor any other passage in the Bible explicitly teaches that unbelievers will be given a "second chance" to believe in Jesus. As 2 Corinthians 6:2 teaches, *"Behold, now is the favorable time; behold, now is the day of salvation."*

10. What do you think life will be like in the new heaven and the new earth?

This is a question which every person will have to answer for himself. In Revelation 21 there are some references to streets of gold, foundations of precious stones and gates of pearl. In Revelation 22 we read some fascinating things about the River of Life which flows from the throne of God. We also read about this throne of God and of the Lamb and our reigning with our Savior for ever and ever. However, neither Revelation 21 or 22 tells us very much about daily living in our new home. Besides, many people believe that the statements in Revelation may be more figurative than literal.

We may be sure, however, that in our eternal home there will be no more suffering, no more sorrow, and no more pain. Disappointments and frustrations will no longer exist. No pure desire will be unmet. No longing will be unfulfilled. There will be no separation from loved ones. No more death. No failures. No sin. And no more night.

On the positive side, we are confident that our future life with Jesus will be far more glorious and wonderful than anything we have ever experienced on earth. We anticipate unending joy and fellowship with our Lord and Savior, activities of one meaningful kind or another that will always provide satisfaction and pleasure, new discoveries which we cannot presently imagine, fellowship with other believers from around the world, and times of glory and blessing that will be richer and deeper than anything we have ever known on earth. Perhaps the Bible doesn't give us many details about our future life since the glory and wonder of living in the new heaven and new earth is so far beyond anything we can imagine that no ordinary words can describe it!

Your Own Salvation

After reading the questions and answers in this Lesson, you may still have some questions about your own personal relationship with Jesus Christ. You may not be sure that your sins have been forgiven. Or you may wonder whether or not you truly are a child of God. Or, perhaps you simply do not know what you should do in order to receive from God the gift of eternal life.

If you sincerely want to commit your life to Christ but are not sure what you should do, I encourage you to humbly and sincerely confess your sins to God, believe with all your heart that Jesus paid the penalty for your sins, and then, in faith, claim God's promise to grant forgiveness and eternal life to all who truly believe.

In order to help you do this, I invite you to pray sincerely the following prayer or a similar prayer of your own.

Dear God, I confess that I have often sinned against you and have not lived the way you want me to live. I have done many things which I should not have done and have failed to do the things which I should have done. Please forgive me. I sincerely believe that Jesus died on the cross in my place and that he rose again for my salvation. In faith I accept from you the gifts of forgiveness and eternal life. With all my heart I thank you for these gifts and, with the help of the Holy Spirit, I promise to love and serve you as long as I live. I pray all of this in the name of my precious Savior, Jesus Christ. Amen!

Read again the promises that God gives to all who confess their sins and put their trust in Jesus for forgiveness and eternal life.

For God so loved the world that he gave his one and only Son, that whoever believes in him shall not perish but have eternal life. (John 3:16)
God has given us eternal life, and this life is in his Son. Whoever has the Son has life; whoever does not have the Son of God does

not have life. . . . I write these things to you who believe in the name of the Son of God so that you may know that you have eternal life. (1 John 5:11-13)

These are the promises of God. Believe and live forever!

About the Author

Dr. Edwin Roels

Education
B.A. Calvin University
M. Div Calvin Theological Seminary
Th.D Free University of Amsterdam

Vocational Highlights
- Professor at Calvin University in Grand Rapids, Michigan
- Professor and Dean of Students at Trinity Christian College in Palos Heights, Illinois
- Civilian chaplain for U.S. servicemen in Seoul, Korea
- Ordained minister in Christian Reformed Churches in South Holland, Illinois and Prinsburg, Minnesota
- Director of Africa programs for the World Home Bible League
- Seminary Professor in India, Romania and Myanmar
- President of Reformed Bible College (now Kuyper College) in Grand Rapids, Michigan
- Author of Bible study materials for the Christian Leaders Institute, World Home Bible League, Crossroads Bible Institute and other mission organizations

E-Professor at Christian Leaders Institute
Dr. Edwin Roels joined the faculty of Christian Leaders Institute in 2012. This book, *What is Christianity?* is named *Christian Basics* in the Course *"Christian Basics: Introduction to Christian Doctrine"* and has been studied by tens of thousands of global Christian leaders.

Made in United States
North Haven, CT
12 December 2024

62261561R00114